MANIFEST
PRESENCE

BOOKS BY DON NORI SR.

Breaking Generational Curses
His Manifest Presence
Hope of a Nation that Prays
How to Find God's Love
Romancing the Divine
Secrets of the Most Holy Place, Volume 1 & 2
Tales of Brokenness
The Angel and the Judgment
The Love Shack
The Prayer God Loves to Answer
You Can Pray in Tongues

AVAILABLE FROM DESTINY IMAGE PUBLISHERS

DON NORI SR.

*M*ANIFEST PRESENCE

You Can Live
Within the Veil

Destiny Image Publishers, Inc.
P.O. Box 351
Shippensburg, PA 17257
"We Publish the Prophets."

This book and all other Destiny Image, Mercy Place, Destiny Image Fiction, and Treasure House books are available at Christian bookstores and distributors worldwide.

For a U.S. bookstore nearest you, call **1-800-722-6774**.
For more information on foreign distributors, call **717-532-3040**.
Reach us on the Internet: **www.destinyimage.com**.

Previously published as ISBN 0-914903-48-9
ISBN-10: 0-7684-2835-1
ISBN-13: 978-0-7684-2835-3

For Worldwide Distribution, Printed in the U.S.A.
1 2 3 4 5 6 7 8 9 10 11 / 13 12 11 10 09

Dedication

To Him who never tires in His pursuit of mere humanity. To Him be the glory forever.

Endorsement

Don Nori not only encourages us to expect *more* of the Manifest Presence of God in our lives, he shows us *how* to *receive* abundantly more of God's fullness than our imaginations can fathom or our expectations can carry us. *Manifest Presence* ignites a compulsion in our hearts to pursue and experience God tangibly with all of our senses. Indeed, Don's book is fragrant with the reality of the cry of God's heart for more of us than before. Be prepared to be catapulted into the greatest of all realms: the realm of the reality of the Father's love.

Todd Bentley
Evangelist/Revivalist

Table of Contents

Introduction

Humankind has always needed security. Indeed, nearly all of humanity's time and personal resources are dedicated to the establishment of those perceived needs that have traditionally been viewed as being able to give peace of mind. These "essentials," it is often believed, are able to shield and protect oneself and one's family from hardship and disaster. In light of this, the energies of most people are focused on preparing for the dire possibilities life might bring to them. Much of humanity's music, philosophy, and religion have also been molded to define, establish, or express the desire for this elusive goal known as security.

But what happens when all manmade securities fail? What happens when all our energies cannot produce even a hope of security, when our philosophies can no longer define our fears, and our religious systems can no longer give us assurance or true inner peace? When these "crutches" begin to deteriorate, individuals find their lives in chaos. As humankind's bastions of security topple, they are left with no hope, no help, and no answer.

It is at this point that the people begin to search for the reality of a living God: a God who transcends philosophies and empty religious traditions, and offers real and tangible solutions in an unraveling world; a God who offers real and lasting security regardless of economic trends, governmental failures, and natural disasters.

When a person begins to see God as a living reality, the theories, philosophical discussions, and religious rituals are then exposed for their shallowness and for their sinister attempts to cover the emptiness and hopelessness of their dogmas. There *is* genuine hope for humankind. There *is* a place of hiding and provision in the middle of life's storms. Our only hope is to find a place of abiding rest in God's Manifest Presence. Our theologies of church planting cannot save us. Our hope is not in the prophetic word or the precision of our worship. It is not based on our calling or our ministry. It is not based on who is in the White House, but rather, it is based on who is in His house.

The externals may serve to draw us into His Presence, but they offer no hope in themselves. When the singers and dancers preceded the children of Israel into battle, it was never the tambourine that caused the enemies to fear. It was God's Manifest Presence that struck fear in the hearts of their enemies. It is the same today.

This book stresses God's desire to dwell with His people in splendid fullness and outlines the provisions we can enjoy through His Presence. It offers practical guidelines for experiencing His Presence and shows how brokenness and purity are essential to true intimacy with God.

As you read these pages, you will discover how God intends David's Tabernacle worship to mature to the fullness of Solomon's Temple, where the glory cloud fell and rulership began.

It is God's desire to manifest His Presence in the midst of His people, but this will happen only as His people learn to seek Him in all His fullness. It is my prayer that this book will bring all the riches of God's Presence into your life and that you might be able to manifest His Presence in all you do.

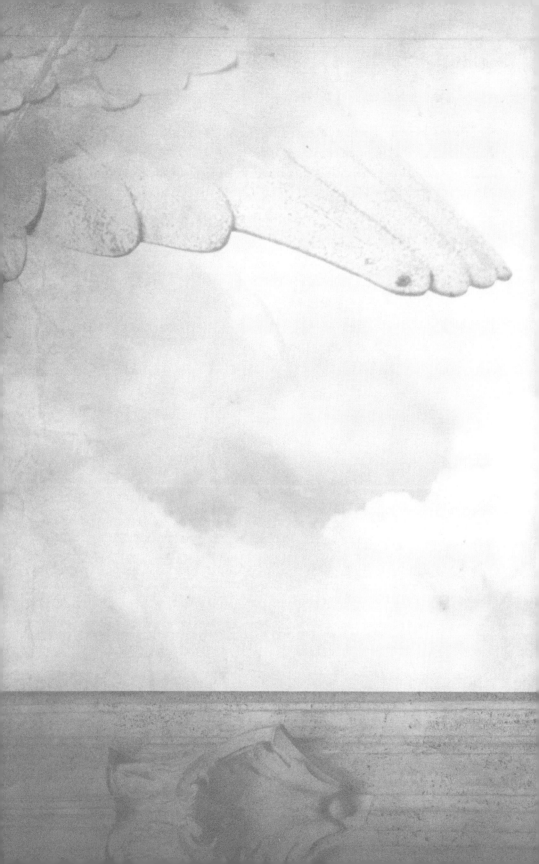

PART I

The Heart Cry of the Lord

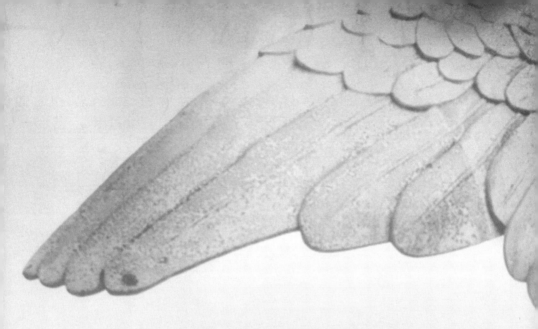

CHAPTER 1

God's Desire—To Dwell With His People

God's Prophetic Word for the Last-Day Church

The Always-Present One will wash away the filth from the women of Jerusalem. He will wash the bloodstains out of Jerusalem. He will cleanse Jerusalem with the spirit of fairness and the spirit of fire. As the Always-Present One did when Israel left Egypt, He will cover them with a cloud of smoke during the day. And, He will cover them with a bright flaming fire at night. These proofs will be over Mount Zion. They will be over every meeting of the people there. There will be a covering over every person. This covering will be a place of safety. It will protect the people from the heat of the sun. It will be a safe place to hide from the storm and rain (Isaiah 4:4-6).

The heat of the day and the storm and rain of the night are coming upon the earth, but God has made a provision for His people that will take them through the times of tribulation that lie ahead. It is not merely coincidental that Isaiah prophesied that a future people would be led by a pillar of fire by night as the Israelites were. Like the Israelites of old, they will also be protected by a canopy of smoke by day.

The canopy and the pillar actually refer to the Manifest Presence of God. This is His prophetic word for the last-day Church; it is the promise of His Manifest Presence going with us. There can be no doubt that it is God's intention and desire to find the remnant of people who will carry His Manifest Presence throughout the earth.

God's Presence

Long ago, God used the prophets to speak to our ancestors many times and in many ways; but, during these last times, God used His Son to speak to us. God appointed him to inherit everything. Through him God made the universe. The Son is the shining brightness of God's glory and the exact picture of God's real being. The Son holds up the universe with his powerful word. After he had provided a cleansing from sin, he sat down at God's right side in heaven (Hebrews 1:1-3).

The Lord is about to visit His temple. Malachi 3:1 says, "Suddenly, the Lord whom you people are looking for* will come to His temple." The Lord is about to come to His temple. He will come suddenly to us. He will walk among us in a real way. When these things take place, we will be able to understand and perceive clearly that God is among us.

There are basically two ways to look at the Presence of God. There is first of all His omnipresence—God is everywhere. We know that God is everywhere, whether we can sense Him or not. God fills the earth. Wherever you go, God will hear your prayer, because His omnipresence covers the earth.

But there is a more specific type of His Presence—His Manifest Presence. God's Manifest Presence is revealed whenever He makes Himself real to *you*, personally. This takes place when He makes Himself real to you *in your spirit* and you know beyond a shadow of a doubt that God has spoken to your heart. You know He has manifested Himself to you; you are experiencing His Manifest Presence.

> GOD'S MANIFEST PRESENCE IS REVEALED WHENEVER HE MAKES HIMSELF REAL TO YOU, PERSONALLY.

God will so fill the Church with His Manifest Presence that He will become perceptible (i.e. tangible) to any or all of our five senses. God manifests Himself in healing. God manifests Himself in change. God manifests Himself in restoration. God manifests Himself in prophecy. Whenever God manifests Himself through any of our natural senses, there is always a visible demonstration that He is literally in the midst of His people.

We walk by faith, not by sight (see 2 Cor. 5:7), but it is not *for* our faith that God chooses to reveal Himself to us. It is rather in *response* to our faith that God manifests Himself. Our faith moves Him to transcend time and space and respond *in* the natural realm to our faith.

God has always delighted in manifesting Himself in a physical, tangible way to His people. His purpose from the very beginning has been to be a manifest God to His people. The entire purpose of redemption was to cleanse for Himself a people to whom He could reveal Himself and with whom He could live in a manifested way. God delights in flowing with and moving with His people.

The dictionary defines *manifest* as: "readily perceived by the senses; easily understood or recognized by the mind; obvious." This is how God wants to make Himself known to us in these last days.

During the day, the Always-Present One went ahead of them in a cloudy column to lead them along the way. During the night, He led them with a fiery column to give them light. They could travel either day or night. The cloudy column during the day or the fiery column during the night was always in front of the people (Exodus 13:21-22).

This is a perfect example of how God manifested Himself to His people.

Another powerful example of God's Manifest Presence is found in Exodus 24:12-18:

Then the Always-Present One said to Moses, "Come up to Me on the mountain and wait there. I will give you the stone plaques, and the commands, which I have written, so that you may teach them to the people." So Moses, along with his assistant, Joshua, got up and went up to the top of the mountain of God. Moses told the elders: "Wait here for us until we return to you. Listen, Aaron and Hur are with you. Whoever has a lawsuit should go to them." Then Moses went up on the mountain. A cloud covered it. The splendor of the Always-Present One settled over Mount Sinai, and the cloud covered it for six days. On the seventh day, God summoned Moses from within the cloud.

The appearance of the glory of the Always-Present One was like a raging fire on top of the mountain in full view of the sons of Israel. And Moses went up on the mountain into the middle of the cloud. He was there on the mountain for 40 days and 40 nights.

Here God manifests Himself audibly and visibly. He is clearly visible to all of Israel.

God manifested Himself to Israel as they went through the wilderness also:

> *On the day that the Holy Tent was set up, God's cloud covered it. The Holy Tent was also called the Tent of the Covenant. From dusk until dawn, the cloud above the Holy Tent looked like fire. The cloud stayed above the Holy Tent. (It looked like fire at night.) Whenever the cloud moved from its position over the Holy Tent, the Israelites moved. Wherever the cloud stopped, that is where the Israelites camped* (Numbers 9:15-17).

God manifested Himself in the midst of His people. It was not an unusual thing to them; it was actually quite common. All the nations of the world had their gods, but Israel was unique in that their God dwelt with them.

ALL THE NATIONS OF THE WORLD HAD THEIR GODS, BUT ISRAEL WAS UNIQUE IN THAT THEIR GOD DWELT WITH THEM.

All the nations of the world would look at Israel and tremble because the God they served was manifested among them. They saw Him; they knew Him. God was in the midst of the children of Israel.

It was God's Manifest Presence in the burning bush on that powerful day when Moses was commissioned to be Israel's deliverer. So mighty was His Presence that God commanded Moses to remove his sandals. "For," the Scriptures declare, "the place where you are standing is holy ground" (Exod. 3:5).

We see God gloriously manifesting His Presence to Solomon in Solomon's Temple. The Presence of the Lord was so visible and so powerful there that the priests could not even minister.

Then all the priests left the sanctuary. All the priests from each group made themselves ready to serve the Always-Present One. All the Levite musicians stood on the east side of the altar. They were Asaph, Heman, Jeduthun, and all their sons and relatives. They were dressed in white linen and played cymbals, lyres, and harps. With them were 120 priests who blew trumpets. Those who blew the trumpets and those who sang together sounded like one person. They praised and thanked the Always-Present One. They sang as they played their trumpets, cymbals, and other instruments. They praised the Always-Present One with this song:

"The Always-Present One is good. His love continues forever!" Then the temple of the Always-Present One was filled with a cloud. The priests could not continue their work because of the cloud. This was because the Always-Present One's glory filled the temple of God (2 Chronicles 5:11-14).

The Lord appeared to Joshua just as he was about to lead the children of Israel into victory over Jericho:

Joshua was near Jericho. He looked up and saw a Man standing in front of him. The Man had a sword in His hand. Joshua went to him and asked, "Are you a friend or an enemy?" The Man answered, "I am neither. I have come now as the Commander of the Always-Present One's army!" Then Joshua laid down on the ground face-down and worshiped Him. Joshua asked, "Do You have a command for me?" The Commander of the Always-Present One's army answered him, "Take off your sandals from your feet, because the place where you are stand-ing is holy." And Joshua did so (Joshua 5:13-15).

It is God's delight to manifest Himself to His people. Here Joshua was about to go into a major battle and was strengthened and encouraged as the angel of the Lord appeared to him. By faith, Joshua would respond to God even without this visitation. The angel of the Lord appeared to him in response to his faith, encouraging him, and confirming his faith all the more.

Moving into the New Testament, we see the Father manifesting Himself to the Church in a variety of a ways. On the Day of Pentecost, God's Presence was manifested with cloven tongues of fire and a rushing, mighty wind sweeping through the place in which the disciples were gathered. God's Presence was so evident that they were able to get in touch with Him through their five senses. What exhilaration and what power energized them from within as they experienced the Manifest Presence of God! (See Acts 2:1-4; 14-38.) Their confidence and assurance in His Presence gave them the ability to preach with great boldness as the Holy Spirit moved upon them with power.

We find Peter and John and the rest of the disciples praying to the Lord for strength and ability in Acts 4:31: "And when they had prayed, the place where they had gathered was shaken, and they were all filled with the Holy Spirit, and began to speak the word of God with boldness." His Manifest Presence transforms mere mortal men, cowering before fleshly strongholds and threats, into mighty men of anointing and power.

> HIS MANIFEST PRESENCE TRANSFORMS
> MERE MORTAL MEN, COWERING BEFORE
> FLESHLY STRONGHOLDS AND THREATS,
> INTO MIGHTY MEN OF ANOINTING AND
> POWER.

We are moving into times when the Manifest Presence of God will be so needed and so great that it will overshadow any of the experiences of the early Church. In fact, the day is coming that we will not even look back at the early Church as a standard for the miraculous because the things that the Lord will be doing in the last-day Church will far exceed what happened in the early Church. Men and women of God will rise up with unprecedented boldness and declare God's Word with great compassion and authority. His Manifest Presence will give them ability and confidence to declare sin to be sin as they witness the Lord Himself confirming their words to the world.

When Stephen was stoned, the Scriptures say that his face shone like that of an angel (see Acts 6:15-7:55). What was that shining but the Manifest Presence of God? Stephen gave over his spirit to the Lord for the sake of the Gospel with victory as God's Presence ushered him into eternity. When Paul was thrown from his horse on the way to Damascus, the Scriptures say that the Word of the Lord came to him. To others it sounded like thunder, but to Paul it was the Manifest Presence of God as he fell before the Lord, repented of his sin, and became a life-long, sold-out disciple for the Lord Jesus Christ (see Acts 9:1-31).

In Acts 12:6, we see the account of Peter sleeping in chains between two guards. When the earth shook, the chains fell from him, and an angel of the Lord appeared to him and directed him out of the prison. (See Acts 12:7-11.)

In our day, we are beginning to see a continual fulfilling of Emmanuel—God with us. God has always desired to live and dwell and manifest Himself in the midst of His people. As He walked with Adam in the cool of the evening (see Gen. 3:8), God also wants to walk with us, so that we will become a people who will experience His Presence, His power, and His glory in a tangible way. The days directly ahead of us will require this. Periods of tribulation and hardship have always driven the people of God into His Presence, thus experiencing His power in mighty ways. Difficult times press God's people into Him so that they, too, will experience His Manifest Presence.

Presence Ponderings

1. The Presence of God is revealed in two ways:

    * His *omnipresence*: God is everywhere.

    * His *Manifest Presence*: God's Presence is revealed when He makes Himself real to you.

2. The perceptibility of God's Presence will increase throughout the coming days as He manifests Himself to His people.

3. As God was in the midst of the children of Israel, so shall He be in the midst of His people today—leading and guiding them with His cloud of glory by day and the fire of His anointing by night.

4. Throughout the New and Old Testaments, God revealed Himself to His people. We are rapidly moving into a time when God's Manifest Presence will become so vital that it will be unlike any experience of the early Church.

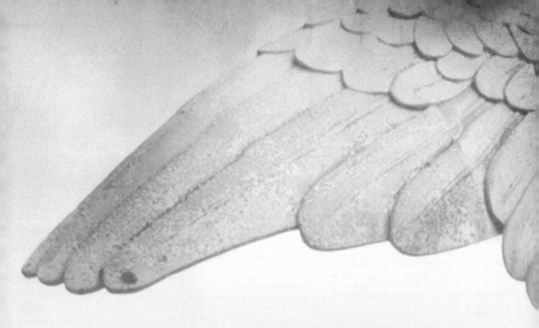

CHAPTER 2

God's Fire—His Means of Preparation

His Presence—Our Only Hope

At that time, the Always-Present One's branch will be very beautiful and great. The people still living in Israel will be proud of what the land grows. All the people who are still living in Jerusalem will be called "holy." This will be all the people whose names are recorded among the living in Jerusalem (Isaiah 4:2-3).

Every single day I find myself recognizing my intense need for the Presence of the Lord Jesus Christ in my life. Every day God shows me my bankruptcy apart from Him. He shows me my total inability to accomplish anything without Him. My hope is in the glory of the Lord.

I used to think of that hope as something that was like my children's hope for a Popsicle before bed. If they get a Popsicle before bed, great. But if they don't, they'll live. More recently, I've realized our hope in the glory of the Lord is not that kind of hope. Our hope is the recognition of our own bankruptcy. Our only hope is that the glory of God will invade us. Our only hope is that the fire of the Presence of God will enter our lives and find a place to abide.

God's Abiding Place

God has always sought a people in whom He could *abide*. We have heard of the visitations of God, but it has never been His intention simply to *visit* His people. He has always looked for a place of *abiding*, where His Presence could dwell permanently.

> GOD HAS ALWAYS SOUGHT A PEOPLE IN WHOM HE COULD *ABIDE*.

In Second Chronicles, when God spoke to Solomon at the dedication of the Temple, God said that He had found a place where His Presence could dwell perpetually (see 2 Chron. 7:16). God is not looking for a place to visit. He is looking for a place to stay. He's looking at your heart and my heart as the permanent dwelling place for His Presence.

I have some relatives who live a few hours away from us. They sometimes come to visit us. For the two or three nights they stay with us, it is a small matter to shuffle the children around so that a bedroom can be made available for the comfort and privacy of our guests during their visit. We all know that their stay will be temporary. We enjoy their visits, so everyone readily endures the minor inconveniences that may be involved. When the relatives pack up and leave, however, everything returns to normal. The children go back to their rooms, and all continues as it was before.

If someone moves into your house to stay, however, the arrangements are obviously quite different. The routine of the household changes *permanently*. Accommodations and adjustments are made on a permanent basis. Having someone come to stay in your own home *permanently* alters your lifestyle. It calls for permanent changes in the routine of how things are done.

In the same way, God wants to come into our hearts to dwell perpetually, to rule and reign through us. He does not come simply to save us, not simply to fill us with His Spirit, but that His Lordship might be manifested, both in us and in all of those around us. Our only hope is for the glory of God to descend upon us and dwell within us. Only then can God have His way in our lives. Only then will we be changed into what God wants us to be. Our hope, our only hope, is for the glory of God to be made manifest.

Such was the dependency of the children of Israel on the Manifest Presence of God. If it hadn't been for the pillar of smoke by day or the column of fire by night, they would not have known where to go, nor could they have survived the wilderness at all! Their guidance was from the Manifest Presence of God. God spoke to them; He showed them the way. Through His Manifest Presence, they could *see* what God was doing.

We serve a God who wants to communicate with His people. We serve a God who wants to be intimate with His people. He doesn't want to pull surprises on us. He wants us to know what He's up to. Jesus said, "I am no longer calling you 'slaves,' because a slave doesn't know what his master is doing. I am calling you 'friends,' because I have revealed to you everything which I have heard from my father" (John 15:15). The Lord is calling us to a place of intimacy where He can speak to us and share His innermost desires with us.

The apostle Paul writes,

> *This gracious love was given to me, even though I am the least important of all the holy people. God wanted to preach the unsearchable*

riches of Christ to non-Jewish people. He wanted to teach everyone about the meaning of the secret plan. It was hidden in God a long, long time ago. (He created everything.) Why was it hidden? So that, through the people whom God called out, His many kinds of wisdom could be made clear to rulers and powers in the heavenly world. This happened for God's eternal purpose which He accomplished in Christ Jesus, our Lord (Ephesians 3:8-11).

God wants to tell us His secrets. The many-faceted wisdom of God that has been hidden for ages and ages contains the very secrets He wants to speak to our hearts. That which is hidden to the rest of creation God wants to manifest to us. Such is the desire in the heart of God to have intimate friendship and fellowship with us.

GOD WANTS TO TELL US HIS SECRETS.

The Israelites could see what God was doing, and they responded to it. When the cloud lifted, they packed their bags and went. And when the cloud descended, they unpacked their bags and remained, no matter if it was for a day, a week, a month, a year. Their hope was in the glory of God. Their hope was in the Manifest of God. Our only hope today is for God to establish His Manifest Presence among us once again.

The Journey of Progressive Revelation

Therefore, we are compelled to continue our pilgrimage in God. We are on a journey of progressive revelation, which will lead us to Him—that where He is, we might also be (see John 14:3). He has prepared a dwelling for us that is pure, holy, and intimate, wholly pleasing to the Father. We must go on as the fathers before us did—

"waiting for a city with foundations that God would design and build" (Heb. 11:10).

Too many Christians look at God and His Word as a neatly categorized pantry closet where everything is predictable. Nothing changes much. But our minds are so inadequate to put God in that kind of order. We are finite; He is infinite. We are natural; He is spiritual. We must understand that dogmatic theology is very often a serious hindrance to progressive revelation. Without progressive revelation, we cannot move forward in His purposes. Thus, we do not move on in God.

The Bible is not a book of doctrine or theology. It is not a closet of neatly arranged doctrines and personal traditions. The Bible is, in essence, a window through which we see Jesus seated at the right hand of God; by gazing through it, we begin to understand the fullness of His desire for us.

> THE BIBLE IS, IN ESSENCE, A WINDOW THROUGH WHICH WE SEE JESUS SEATED AT THE RIGHT HAND OF GOD; BY GAZING THROUGH IT, WE BEGIN TO UNDERSTAND THE FULLNESS OF HIS DESIRE FOR US.

Certainly, all we believe and accept as truth must be in harmony with and be proven by the Bible. But progressive revelation demands flexibility. There is a difference between my own carnal insight and divine revelation. I must be open to new light from the Word if I am to grow into and experience the fullness of His Manifest Presence.

As glorious as David's Tabernacle was, it was not the final resting place for the Presence of God. History compels us to understand that

God's fullness, represented by the glory cloud, never fell in David's Tabernacle. Once the ark was stolen by the Philistines from Moses' Tabernacle, the cloud of glory never fell on it again.

Therefore, let us move on, not falling into the trap of many past movements of camping around an issue or a doctrine, but rather moving on into His ravishing fullness as it is displayed by Solomon's Temple. There His unabashed Presence fills all in all and beckons us today to come and experience Him in utter completeness and wholeness. There, the sweetness of fellowship with the living God reaches its ultimate ability to minister to our soul and body. There we come to understand David's declaration in Psalm 73:16-17, "I tried to understand all of this, but it was too much for me to stand, until I went to the sanctuary of God! Then I understood what will happen to them [wicked men]." There, the instruction of the Lord and the learning and walking in His ways will be fulfilled as prophesied by Micah:

> *Many nations will come and say: "Come, let us go up to the mountain of the Always-Present One, and to the temple of the God of Jacob! Then God will teach us from His ways. And, we will live by His paths." His teachings will go forth from Zion. The message of the Always-Present One will go out from Jerusalem* (Micah 4:2).

God intends this to be the most powerful of relationships! But there is a price to pay. And the price tag is steep—it demands your life! "He who has found his life shall lose it, and he who has lost his life for My sake shall find it" (Matt. 10:39). We will learn how one goes about paying this price and just what will happen when one decides there is nothing else worth living for and freely pays it.

I am not at all suggesting that the ornate natural beauty of the temple is that to which God responds today. He wants a *spiritual habitation* as glorious as Solomon's Temple. No wonder "we are His workman-ship" (see Eph. 2:10). The gold, silver, and precious stones should be within our hearts.

The Need to Be Flexible

My work enables me to talk to people around the world. Every-one I talk to says we're on the verge of a great outpouring of the Holy Spirit and great revival. If we want to be used, we must keep our wineskins soft. We have to let God change us. We have to be dili-gent, not permitting ourselves to get into ruts. We can never be satis-fied with just existing. Bored Christians are unchanging Christians. Bored Christians are not involved with God. Bored Christians are usually stubborn Christians, unwilling or unable to hear His voice. Those who are soft and pliable and quiet before God are the busiest and most fulfilled people on earth.

His glory comes when we stay soft. This enables us to change. When God comes into His Church, or an individual believer's life, everything has to change. For a period of time, it may seem that God is not doing anything right. He will upset our doctrines and change things about our worship and our methods. When God comes to His people, the historical pattern shows us that *everything changes*.

We should be looking for God to manifest Himself among us, not with just an occasional visitation, but with His abiding Presence, His abiding love, and His abiding anointing on our lives.

> WHEN GOD COMES INTO HIS CHURCH, OR AN INDIVIDUAL BELIEVER'S LIFE, *EVERY-THING* HAS TO CHANGE.

God is getting ready "to upset the apple cart." He will cause so many things to happen that simply don't fit with our preconceived ideas. But God is on the move and I believe He will establish His Presence within us. The Presence of God will become so manifest in the midst of His people that healing and restoration will come as someone brings forth a word, or in a time of worship, or just as people pray for one another. To a degree, this is already happening, but there will soon be a great acceleration of this kind of activity. There will be a sense of His Presence that is so real that we won't have to convince one another that God is here. God will manifest Himself in the midst of the assembly.

> THERE WILL BE A SENSE OF HIS PRESENCE THAT IS SO REAL THAT WE WON'T HAVE TO CONVINCE ONE ANOTHER THAT GOD IS HERE.

His Manifest Presence may not take the form of a literal fire by night or a literal smoke by day, but it will be a reality nonetheless. The children of Israel could look at the Manifest Presence of God and say, "There is God," and so will we be able to do. God will so move in the midst of His people that we will be able to say, "God is moving, and there He is."

But there's more to it than just this. God will manifest Himself to the nations as well. How else, as the prophet Isaiah said, will the nations stream to the light? (See Isaiah 60:3.)

God will show Himself to a people who love Him, and He's going to show Himself *through* a people who love Him. The eyes of the world will see Him, whether they're believers or nonbelievers. He will make believers out of people when He manifests Himself through those whom He has called to Himself in these last days.

The time is coming when chaos and hardship will be everywhere. Manmade dogmas and institutions will topple around us. There will be no place of safety. Everyone will be looking for a place of shelter, a place to hide. The Bible says that some will run to the hills and go to the mountains, and some will run into caves; and some won't be able to find any place to hide and they'll beg the trees and rocks to fall on them to deliver them from fear and turmoil (see Rev. 6:16). But God's people have a refuge. God's people will have a shelter from the storm that is soon to come upon the earth. That shelter is the very Presence of the Most High God. As the Psalmist said, "Because You are my Help, I will gladly sing of Your protection" (Ps. 63:7). God's people will need to find this place of rest. They'll need to find His Manifest Presence as a place of shelter if they are to endure that which is coming upon the earth.

Erasing Our "Pencil Principles"

Have you ever heard of "pencil principles"? They are traditions and methods that are currently helpful in our understanding and response to the Lord. "Pencil principles" are not doctrines and can therefore be easily replaced.

A serious problem arises when we begin to think these temporary principles or "helps" are God's final thoughts on an issue. For instance, many churches have been using LCD projectors to display the words of songs during worship and praise. But can we hear the Lord if, for some reason, He would want a songbook instead?

Meeting times and Bible studies are another example. A Tuesday morning women's group may be a vital tool for a season in God's economy. But it would be a mistake to make it a requirement for all emerging churches. The Tuesday meeting was a "pencil principle," a need for the moment that might never exist again.

There are "pencil principles" that we follow in our worship and in other areas of our lives that may need to be erased when the Manifest Presence of God comes. These "principles" may be good for a season, but when God comes to us and changes the order of things, we should be able to erase outdated principles easily without stubbornly holding them dear; for God is always moving us onward. These externals change as often as the scenery changes while we are traveling down the highway.

We're living in a time of great excitement and great anticipation. God is about to move upon us. Just as God manifested Himself in the days of Israel, so He wants to manifest Himself today in reality. "O Jerusalem, get up and shine. Your light has come. The splendor of the Always-Present One shines on you" (Isa. 60:1). When the glory of the Lord rises upon the Church, it will be visible. People will know that God is in the midst of His people. "For behold, darkness will cover the earth, and deep darkness the peoples; but the Lord will rise upon you, and His glory will appear upon you. And nations will come to your light, and kings to the brightness of your rising" (Isa. 60:2-3 NKJV).

This isn't a fairytale! It will happen! This *is* happening! Darkness covers the deep, and gross darkness covers the people. But the glory of the Lord will rise upon the Church. The nations will come to its light. Our hope is not in pencil principles! Our hope for revival cannot be found in a program.

The days of religious counterfeiting are coming abruptly to an end. The days of being able to say we believe something and yet live like we don't believe it are fast coming to a close, because the difficulty of the times we live in will reveal our hypocrisy. The day of religious falsehood is rapidly coming to an ending, as men and women around the world seek reality. The only way we will be able to survive is to find the true and living God, to discover the true and living tabernacle, the very Presence of God as our refuge.

In that day, a person's ability as a choir director will not help. Someone's ability as a talented musician or worship leader will not help. An artist's ability to create the most fantastic banners or someone's ability to create the most spectacular dances in the Spirit will not help. Only God is the help of our lives. And His Presence is that which will shelter us and give us strength.

We will need to experience the miraculous power of God moment by moment. That will come only through an abiding, intimate relationship with Him. These are the days when we must seek the Lord while He may be found, when we must conform to His will and His desires and allow His Spirit to change us from glory to glory, so that we will be able to stand in the days ahead. Our only hope for revival, for restoration, for an outpouring of the Holy Spirit, is for God to establish His glory among His people.

One of the greatest things I've learned about the Lord is that He doesn't like His people to be in a rut. As soon as He sees people saying, "Well, this is the way it was done this Sunday, and this is the way we'll do it next Sunday," or "This is the way I taught a Bible study this year, so this is the way we'll do it next year," He comes in and changes things around—because He is the One who wants to make the decisions; He is the One who chooses.

> ONE OF THE GREATEST THINGS I'VE LEARNED ABOUT THE LORD IS THAT HE DOESN'T LIKE HIS PEOPLE TO BE IN A RUT.

When His glory rises in the Church, there will be a people who will simply respond to Him by saying, "God, do whatever you want to do." God's people won't argue with Him. They won't be bound by their own traditions and pet doctrines. They're not going to hold their own opinions so dear that God will not be able to speak to them.

The People of His Presence

The people God is raising up will be able to discern the difference between their own traditions and the will of God. They will discern between the doctrines of men and the doctrines of the Lord, and they will lay down the doctrines of men to fulfill the will of God. They are not captive to denominational or charismatic "streams." They hear the Word of the Lord and allow the Word of the Lord to change their direction. They move purely on what God says to them.

Isaiah said that nations will *run* to the light. God doesn't just tell us stories to give us the strength to go from one week to the next. These are events, points in time, prophecies about you and me, about the last-day Church; and these prophecies *will* come to pass, just as God spoke through the prophets, and what they spoke forth came to pass. God is still speaking through the prophets, and His Word is still coming to pass. The glory of the Lord will rise upon the Church. The Manifest Presence of God will be established in the midst of the people. "Nations will come to your light. Kings will come to the brightness of your sunrise" (Isa. 60:3).

The Burning of the Chaff

Because I love Jerusalem, I will continue to speak [on her behalf].
For Jerusalem's sake, I will not stop speaking. I will speak until

her goodness shines like a bright light. I will speak until her salvation burns bright like a flame (Isaiah 62:1).

God wants to light up your life with His Presence. He wants to set you on fire. Our salvation will be "like a torch that is burning."

The Always-Present One has chosen Jerusalem. He wants it for His home. He says: "This is my resting-place forever. Here is where I want to stay. I will bless her with plenty of nourishment. I will satisfy her poor people with food. I will let her priests receive deliverance. And, those of her who follow God will truly sing for joy! There [in Jerusalem] I will make a king come from the family of David. For My anointed one, I will provide a descendant" (Psalm 132:13-17).

Who is the lamp for His anointed? It's us! We are the lamp for His anointed, predestined to carry His flame.

The glory of the Lord must rise upon the people. He will break through our carnal thought processes. He will break through our humanism. He will break though our ruts. He will break through our lackadaisical attitudes. He will break through our "middle classism." And He will break through our mere existence, so that He might come through with what He wants to do in His glory and His righteousness and His purposes.

The Lord will burn away the chaff in our lives until only the wheat remains. He will consume the flesh with His fire so that the spiritual can come forth. In this way, we will be able to witness His Presence.

Peter says, "We saw His greatness!" (2 Pet. 1:16). There are over 50 references either to the Church being the witness of what God was doing or of Israel being the witness of God. The Bible gives us more than 50 references of man witnessing the Manifest Presence of God. When God says, "You will be My witnesses," what is it that we are to be witnesses of? Not of a doctrine. Not of a system. But of Him. We are witnesses of *Him*. John came to bear witness of Jesus (see Matt. 11:10). Jesus said that He only spoke what the Father said and He only did what He saw His heavenly Father doing (see John 8:28).

Every time we're called upon to be His witnesses, we are witnesses of reality. We are witnesses of Him. We are witnesses of God's Manifest Presence. We cannot possibly compete with this world's system. If we try to win the world for Jesus Christ through this world's system, we won't succeed. We don't have the money or the resources or the mental abilities to launch the kind of campaign it would take to even make a dent in this world. Our only hope is for the Scriptures to come to pass. Our only hope is for the Presence of God to find His resting place, His final abode among His people.

Omnipresence or Manifest Presence?

The time has come for us to change our emphasis from God's omnipresence to His Manifest Presence. It's so easy to say, "Yes, God is here." Anybody can say that, because *God is here.* But when God manifests Himself to you, He is "here" in an entirely new way! We know He is "here" because He speaks to us, because He moves in our hearts, because lives are changed, because I see and touch and feel Him.

> THE TIME HAS COME FOR US TO CHANGE OUR EMPHASIS FROM GOD'S OMNIPRESENCE TO HIS MANIFEST PRESENCE.

God waits to show Himself in His wonderful fullness to the Church. It will happen as soon as the Church that Jesus is building comes forth with eager anticipation of His fullness. The world is perishing for lack of the Church that Jesus is building, and we are famishing for His Presence. We have, so long, been satisfied with principles—even charismatic principles—that sometimes I think we've lost our heartthrob for Him, for His Presence, for His Word to us, for His comfort to us.

I know I was created for His praise. I'm created to bring Him pleasure. But I want you to know it brings Him pleasure whenever He can comfort us. It gives Him pleasure when He knows there's a people who will embrace Him and love Him and whom He can love in return.

God's heart is at the threshold of the Church. He is yearning, even crying for a people who will say, "Come, Lord Jesus, into our midst. Come, Lord Jesus, and just do whatever you want to do. Break through my theology, break through my carnality, break through my human desires, break through my human will, break through all this stuff that holds me earth-bound. God, have your way in me! Come and manifest Yourself in my life!" In response to that prayer, He comes and sets us on fire.

He wants to have a Church, a people upon whom His glory can rest. He wants to have a lamp for His anointed to which the nations can flee. His plan is to prepare for Himself a habitation, and that is the Church.

He will do it by baptizing, or immersing, His people into Himself by the Holy Spirit and by fire.

John said, "I immerse you in water, but there is One coming who is more important than I am. I am not worthy to untie His shoe. He will immerse you in the Holy Spirit and in fire" (Luke 3:16). We know what the baptism in the Holy Spirit is about, and we like to talk about it and embrace it. We know that the baptism in the Holy Spirit provides us with the empowering of the gifts and the empowering to witness and the power to strengthen us. It also supplies us with those things that are necessary for creating His life in us and for developing the ministries that are within us. We embrace wholeheartedly these aspects of the Holy Spirit. However, we must also embrace the fact that the baptism of *fire* is also His Presence. The fire is the Lord. We are amazed by the power of a fire when we look at a pile of wood burning or we see a house burning down. It's so terrible and awesome. Fire can be a very ruthless and destructive force. This is all too frequently our only concept of fire.

The writer of Hebrews tells us, "...our God is a like a fire which destroys everything" (Heb. 12:29). We may not understand that God is not to be viewed as a destructive fire. He is not a ruthless burner of everything that's in our lives, good or bad. He is the fire, but His is a controlled fire, an orderly fire, a purposeful fire. It has specific reasons for burning. It has specific reasons for being set inside of us. It does not burn the precious. It just burns the dross.

It is well for us to remember that the only thing that cannot be affected by fire is that which has already been burned. Pure gold is only softened by fire. It cannot become more pure. Whatever is not pure, however, needs the fire. The only thing that *can* burn is that which *hasn't yet* been burned.

God wants to have a place where He can manifest His glory. And His plan is to do it by planting Himself in you and me. I've stopped saying, "There's fire in my life," because He *is* my life. He is manifesting His Presence in my life when He is burning the dross from me. He is manifesting Himself in us when we say we're burning in the furnace of affliction. It is He who is at work in our lives. It is His Person manifesting Himself to us. He is the fire.

HE IS MANIFESTING HIS PRESENCE IN MY
LIFE WHEN HE IS BURNING THE DROSS
FROM ME.

Prepared for Tribulation

The sinners in Jerusalem are afraid. The people who are sepa-rated from God shake with fear. They say: "Can any of us live through this fire that destroys? Who can live near this fire that burns on and on?" A person might do what is right. He might speak what is right. He might refuse to take money unfairly. He might refuse to take money to hurt others. He might not listen to plans of murder. He might refuse to think about evil (Isaiah 33:14-15).

There was a time when I thought these verses were talking about hell.

I could not understand the relationship between the two verses. I asked God why these people would be dwelling in the fire. Who will be able to dwell with the perpetual fires and the everlasting burnings?

He showed me that He is the fire. Those who walk righteously will be able to dwell with Him. When judgment comes, who will be able to stand unaffected?

Who are the ones who will be able to be God's witnesses in the time of tribulation? It will be those who have already been changed by the fire; those who have already been purified by burning. Those are the ones who will be able to stand.

We have our choice as to when we want to face the fire. We can face the fire during times of tribulation that God brings upon us, or we can face the fire when the world faces it in the time to come. The people who will stand and be used of the Lord are those who, as the Old Testament prophet says, "look like torches" (see Nahum 2:4), those who have allowed judgment to come upon them first. These are the people who will allow the Holy Spirit to change them, to work in their hearts to burn out the dross, to burn out the sin, to burn out even the things that weren't necessarily sin except that they held them back from the Presence and purposes of God.

Even the good things we like to do and enjoy oftentimes need to be purged from our lives because they take away from God's purposes. God so works in our hearts and so establishes His glory and His love and His life within us that we say, "God, whatever you want to do, go ahead and do it."

He is the purger. He is the purifier. He is the cleanser. He is the smelter. God is the fire. The fire makes us holy. The heat purifies the heart.

This is a statement of the Always-Present One to my Lord: "Sit at My right side until I put your enemies under your control." The Always-Present One will make you King in Jerusalem over all nations. And, you will rule over your enemies. Your people will join you on the day when you come to power. You have been dressed in holiness from birth. You have the freshness of a child (Psalm 110:1-3).

Have we reached the point where we can say, "I would rather have God's Presence in my life manifested in fire than not at all"? Our God is a consuming fire. He wants to have a people in whom He can establish His glory. Our response needs to be the same as that of David, who said, "Let us go into His dwelling place; let us worship at His footstool" (Ps. 132:7).

If we're wondering why we're not changing, if we're wondering why there seems to be no anointing, we have to ask ourselves, "Is there no burning? Are we protecting our self-life? Are we protecting the *me*? Are we protecting the sin? Are we protecting whatever it is that God wants to deal with?"

To burn is to grow. And to burn with His Presence is to be aglow with His Spirit. It's not just a big charismatic smile. It is the fire of God burning in us that produces the life and the smile that radiates with God's Presence. This will produce a willing people in the "day of His power," the "day of holiness."

> IT IS THE FIRE OF GOD BURNING IN US
> THAT PRODUCES THE LIFE AND THE SMILE
> THAT RADIATES WITH GOD'S PRESENCE.

A Lamp for His Anointed

He wants to have "a lamp for His anointed." His plan is to prepare His people to be that lamp. Our response must be, "Lord, do it. Burn away the dross. Teach me to respond to you when I am offended. Teach me to respond to you when I am wronged. Teach me to respond to you in every situation." The result will be a willing and prepared people whom God can use.

God is beginning to establish that kind of reality in us so that His Presence is manifest within us. When we know that God is in something, how can it be bad? Even when I lose, I win. Even when I blow it, I profit. So there's only hope for us.

49

Whether it be in the form of a dove or in fire, God wants to establish Himself in us so that His Presence will be manifested. It can be in the church, and it can also be in our homes and in our jobs. When it happens, people will look at you and see Jesus—not because you preach to them, but because your life radiates His Manifest Presence. God is manifesting Himself to us. This Manifest Presence is what will bring the nations to the Church.

It is His Manifest Presence that protects us. It's His Manifest Presence that gives us the peace of mind and peace of heart to know that "At your side, 1,000 people may die, or even 10,000 right beside you, but You will not be hurt!" (Ps. 91:7).

This, then, is my peace, and this, then, is my rest. It does not come from some mental assent of God's being everywhere, of His Presence being everywhere, nor is it just intellectually agreeing with that statement. It is emotionally, personally, and spiritually experiencing His Presence in the kind of reality that says, "I know that I know that I know that Jesus Christ is with me." "Since God is for us, who can be against us?" (Rom. 8:31). "The Lord is my helper, I will not be afraid. What can man do to me?" (Heb. 13:6). As you trust in Jesus, His Presence will increase in your life far beyond what you could ever ask or imagine.

Presence Ponderings

1. Our hope is in the glory of the Lord and that He may find a place of permanence in our lives for His manifest Presence to abide.

2. God wants to reveal His venerable knowledge and manifest the inner-most secrets of His heart to His people.

3. We must move in the spirit according to God's ravishing fullness, as displayed by Solomon's Temple. We must not repeat history's mistakes of camping around doctrinal issues but instead prepare to experience the fullness of God.

4. God is raising up people who will run to the light of His glory. His glory is breaking through our carnal thought-processes and preparing the way for His purpose and power in our lives to be revealed.

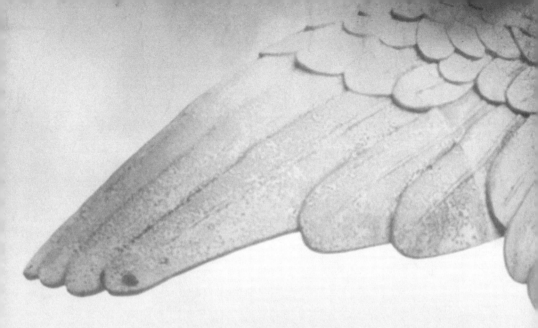

CHAPTER 3

God's Ministry—From the Sanctuary

This is the point of what is being said: We have such a High Priest. He sat down in heaven at the right side of God's throne. He is a Minister in the most holy place, the tent which is real. God, not man, put up this tent (Hebrews 8:1-2).

As God's Word comes forth from Zion (the people of God—His Church), its purpose is to effect changes in our lives. God wants to impart so many things to us. The real "bottom line" in our Christian walk is not how well we sing or prophesy or preach or how many hours a day we serve the people. It's how soft our hearts are before the Lord. We must ask ourselves, "How am I changing before Him?" Our ultimate service is before Him, not before the pastor or the people. When we really understand that our service is unto Him, we realize that He sees us all the time, whether we're at home by ourselves, or at work, or wherever we may be. Whenever I am serving Him, my lifestyle reflects His love.

The King Is Coming to His Sanctuary

God has never intended His Church to be without a King. He has never intended the throne room of the holy of holies (our hearts) to be unoccupied. His intention from the very beginning was for the King to dwell there, to have His throne in the midst of His people.

Now one thing we know for certain is that He *will have* a people who will allow Him to dwell within them. That people might be small or great in number; they may appear to be light-years ahead of everybody else. But they are people who are satisfied with nothing less than God's abiding Presence.

They will not give up; they are not quitters. They're not satisfied with anything less than all that God has for them. Whether that band of people in a particular town consists of ten or twenty or fifty or one hundred, the prerequisite they've discovered is that *God will work with broken hearts*. He will work through hearts that are open and soft in their response to Him. He'll work through hearts that are flexible. He will work through people who are willing to have their plans changed, who are willing to have their careers changed, who are willing to have their homes changed, who are willing to have anything changed for the sake of serving God. Those are the people in whom God will establish His throne. And those are the people in whom God *is establishing* His throne today.

One Sunday night, as I was taking my walk with the Lord in the fields behind my home, I started to thank the Lord for the flow of the Spirit we enjoyed in church that morning. I had felt there was a really significant prophetic flow in song and prophecy and the reading of the Scriptures. It seemed so powerful and meaningful! As I walked along the railroad tracks, I thanked the Lord for the morning meeting, and I told Him how much I appreciated His Presence with us: "Lord, thank you for the flow of your Spirit."

The Holy Spirit responded in a surprising way, *"What flow?"*

I explained, "The flow of your Spirit this morning in church."

The Lord countered my statement with, *"There wasn't a flow, Don. What you thought was a flow was actually the lifting of the people into a significant area of My sanctuary. There is no flow there; it is a place where you see!"*

On that memorable autumn evening I learned an important truth. The flow of the Spirit in the sanctuary of God's Presence is like a flashlight in a darkened room. As you sweep the room with the flashlight, you might say, "Oh, there I can see a picture hanging on the wall. And over there I can make out a piano." As the flashlight continues to sweep around the room, you would be able to find individual pieces of furniture—chairs, a table, a lamp, a bookcase. But you could only see where the flashlight was shining at a given time and in a given direction.

The Fullness of the Sanctuary

Walking in the fullness of the sanctuary, however, is like having the overhead light in the room turned on so that you can see everything in its proper context, not in segments or pieces. In the sanctuary, you "know even as you are known." What we experienced that Sunday morning was not a flow where people were following a flashlight, but the overhead light was on and people were talking about what they were seeing.

Life with only a flashlight is very limited, isn't it? And if there are people who are living according to the flashlight principle, they are not living in real fullness. Their vision and understanding are limited to a single beam of light. When we are ministering from God's fullness, however, the floodlights are on, and we see and perceive in fullness.

> WHEN WE ARE MINISTERING FROM GOD'S FULLNESS HOWEVER, THE FLOODLIGHTS ARE ON, AND WE SEE AND PERCEIVE IN FULLNESS.

God wants to establish His throne and His sanctuary within us. The Scriptures say, "This is what the Always-Present One of the armies [of heaven] says: "I have a very strong love for Zion. I love her intensely!" (Zech. 8:2).

God is jealous for His Church. When we act in immature, childish, and petty ways, we resist God's Presence. Those actions deny the fact that He is alive within us. If we intend to be His people, we have to be people who have a lifestyle that draws God to us. Our actions should not make the world think that He is not with us at all.

"This is what the Always-Present One says: 'I will return to Zion. I will dwell inside Jerusalem. Then it will be called "the City of Truth." And the mountain of the Always-Present One of the armies [of heaven] will be called "the Holy Mountain"'" (Zech. 8:3). Many folks live one way in church and another way at home. What hypocrisy! God is in our homes as well as in our churches. He always sees our actions and knows our thoughts. The old carnal religious system tells us that kind of hypocritical behavior is acceptable. When we are in Christ, however, such behavior denies God's Presence and power in our lives. It dilutes His anointing within and ruins our witness. On the other hand, there are those who love God for His sake alone. They obey Him even when no one can see their actions. They have "truth in their innermost being." God will dwell in those hearts. He will manifest Himself in mighty ways through those lives.

Zion—The Place Where God Dwells

There is a song that declares: "Awake, O Israel, put off your slumber, for the Lord has set you free. For out of Zion comes your Redeemer in the year of Jubilee." It's interesting that Israel is the type of the Church, but Zion is the type of the dwelling place of God. Zion was the holy hill. It was a hill in the middle of Jerusalem, and Jerusalem was in the middle of Israel. Zion was where the sanctuary of God was. Zion *was* the sanctuary of God. Mount Zion was where David's Tabernacle was situated. That was where there was free access into the Presence of God.

The only way for Israel to be filled with God was if the Presence of God came out of Zion. He wouldn't come through Samaria. He wouldn't come by means of a spaceship. He wouldn't come through Persia. The Presence and power and anointing of God had to come through Mount Zion. When God's Presence was established in Mount Zion, all Israel would be filled with His Presence. The sanctuary of God was Mount Zion. And when God's sanctuary is established in Mount Zion, the whole Church will be filled with His Presence.

The promise of the Lord through Zechariah is: "I will return to Zion and will dwell in the midst of Jerusalem." (See Zechariah 8:3.) The Presence of God dwelling on Mount Zion means He was in the middle of Jerusalem. We talk about wanting to enter God's sanctuary, and wanting to minister from His sanctuary, but where is God's sanctuary today?

God dwells within me. If I am to minister from the sanctuary, I must minister from my heart. That's why there has been such a call for the Church to return to holiness. That's why there's such a call to return to purity, to be soft, to be flexible, to be pliable.

The ministry of the sanctuary is the ministry from the heart. It's that which comes from the depths of my heart, where Jesus Christ dwells. For Jesus to dwell in you, there has to be a place deep inside of you that is pure. *His sanctuary is within you.* That's why Jesus says, "Behold, why are you looking here and looking there and over there? The Kingdom of God is within you" (see Luke 17:21—author's paraphrase).

For several months before I was saved, I experienced a burning deep inside that impelled me to respond to God. This burning sensation eventually caused me to give in to God's Spirit. It happened when this thought came to me: *"Follow your heart.* Give in to your heart's desire." When I followed that advice, I came to Jesus.

As long as I give myself to Him, and as long as I follow my heart, I find myself witnessing, serving the Lord, serving other people, praying for people. This happens as long as I am ministering from my heart, from where Jesus dwells.

Ministering From Our Hearts

God wants us to be people who respond according to our hearts. Someone has said, "When a person gets filled with the Holy Spirit, you need to cage him up for three months, because he's not ready for service. A newly Spirit-filled person just goes crazy for three months at least." The truth is, however, that when you first yield your heart to Jesus you are soft before Him. In all likelihood, therefore, instead of locking a new believer up, you should push him out into the streets. He'll probably minister closer to the heart of God than he will six months later.

> GOD WANTS US TO BE PEOPLE WHO RE-SPOND ACCORDING TO OUR HEARTS.

When we first repent of our sins and give our hearts to the Lord, we say, "God, change me. God, transform me." God responds, and a mighty change takes place within. We're simply motivated by our hearts, and we serve the Lord by witnessing fervently and telling others about Jesus. We tell almost everyone we see about all the great things that are happening to us and through us. We witness miracles in our daily lives. That's because we're ministering from our hearts where all we see is Jesus.

Then what happens? We start seeing ourselves again. We start seeing our own problems; we start seeing our own needs. Our selfishness begins creeping back in. The old sin of our lives starts to creep back in.

Then, all of a sudden, we calm down. The people around us may say, "Great! He's finally settling down." Often, the reason we settle down is because carnality and religion have entered back in.

Where carnality doesn't enter in, there is a bubbling over of God's life and Presence. In such a life, God's power continues to grow and bubble up until everything is flooded with His life and His Presence.

Keeping Our Hearts Before God

We must keep our hearts like we keep a garden. In starting a garden, we drop the plow blade or rototiller arms into the earth and we tear the ground up in preparation for the time when we will let God take over. We get out all the rocks and remove other debris. We plant tomatoes, peppers, onions, lettuce, radishes, cucumbers, and squash, and start watering our potential garden. As the plants begin to grow, so do the weeds.

We may observe, "I got rid of that weed last week. Why am I letting it grow in my garden again?" Your response is to get in there and pull out those weeds. On and on it goes until the time of harvest comes.

The same is true in our spiritual lives. We may say, "I got rid of that sin the day I got saved. Why is it still in my garden?" You respond by pulling it out. But sometimes the weeds of sin and complacency threaten to take over.

We need to keep our hearts like we keep a garden. We must not put off the need for weed-pulling. Our repentance must be immediate each time we see a weed of sin emerging. It is our responsibility to get out there and pull those weeds. If we don't, they will get bigger and bigger and bigger, and all of a sudden they will take over the tomatoes and peppers and start choking out the life of the fruits and vegetables we wish to produce.

> WE NEED TO KEEP OUR HEARTS LIKE WE KEEP A GARDEN.

We need to be people who are not people of excuses: "Well, I can't serve God now because…" Or, "I can't take my time with God now because…" "I don't have time to pray because…" "I don't have time to tend my garden because…" In such a life, the weeds are still growing. The end result will be that that person will miss the feast.

This is especially true for those who are in ministry. For you not to keep your heart like a garden is very dangerous. It takes time to cultivate; it takes time to weed; it takes time to diligently and daily seek the Lord and to allow the Holy Spirit to show us where the weeds are so that we can get in there and pull them out (see Matt. 13:24-30).

God wants us to be a people who are ready to serve the Lord Jesus, a people who are fit to be called *His*, a people who are fit to minister from the sanctuary, *from His sanctuary*, which is our hearts.

Here-and-Now Provision of Genuine Salvation

Let's look again at Psalm 132.

The Always-Present One has chosen Jerusalem. He wants it for His home. I will bless her (the city of Jerusalem) with plenty of nourishment. I will satisfy her poor people with food (Psalm 132:13,15).

This familiar verse doesn't say He will take His priests to Heaven in order to bless them. He will bring Heaven down and clothe His priests with salvation right here on earth. God's intention is not just to get you to Heaven. As you begin to understand that you are a priest of God, you will realize that His purpose is to clothe you with salvation. You wear salvation like clothing. It's visible. It's something people will see. It's something that will draw people to God. We are clothed with His salvation.

That spiritual clothing will become more and more manifest (or obvious) as the days go on. You will be clothed with the very salvation of God. You will be carrying His salvation to the four corners of the earth. Your preaching of repentance will not be to have people simply go to Heaven. It will be, "Repent, and here's salvation coming to you."

The promise of our marriage to the Lamb is not something that will happen when we die. How would you like to get engaged and not be able to get married until you die? Isn't that absurd? Doesn't the Bible teach us that the relationship between the husband and wife is like the relationship between Christ and the Church? If that's true, then our lifestyles should be as though we're married to Him *now*. The blessings and the salvation that come with being married to the Lamb should be our experience in the here and now, shouldn't it? If not, we can cancel the wedding, because we'll get married in Heaven.

"I will abundantly bless her provision; I will satisfy her needy with bread. And I will clothe her priests with salvation, and her saints will shout for joy" (Ps. 132:15). That's for right now—here in *this life*. In this life, we are to be bearers of the salvation of God.

It is certain that all persons die one time. And, the Judgment Day comes after death. In the same way, Christ was sacrificed once for all time to take away the sins of many people. Christ will come again. Why? Not to get rid of sin, but to save people who are waiting for Him. They will see Him (Hebrews 9:27-28).

Purifying Our Hearts for Spiritual Growth

James 3:11 says, "Does good water and bitter water flow from the same fountain?" We need to purify our hearts. We need to purify His sanctuary within us so that whenever He comes forth, He comes in His fullness. Nothing bitter or hateful comes with Him.

"...the sacrifice that God wants is a broken (yielding) spirit. O God, You will not reject a heart that is broken and sorry for its sin" (Ps. 51:17). Whenever we are broken, our hearts become teachable. When our hearts are broken, we're soft. We can take change. We can take input into our lives. We can take pastoral care. We can take hearing a word from the Lord from a friend, even if it's a word of rebuke. When our hearts are not contrite, we cannot respond to correction, input, and the purification of the Holy Spirit. It is impossible to respond to Him when we always think we're right or that a particular admonition is ridiculous. If we treat one another that way, we are treating Him that way, too.

> **WHENEVER WE ARE BROKEN, OUR HEARTS BECOME TEACHABLE.**

The Scriptures say, "If you can't love your brother you can see, you can't love God whom you can't see. And if you can't respond to your brother you can see, you cannot respond to God whom you can't see" (1 John 4:20—author's paraphrase). People may say, "Well,

I don't listen to man; I just listen to God." If this is the case, you miss a lot of what God has to say, and you have a rebellious spirit.

I was saved less than a year when I was invited to give my testimony at a church in a town where I went to college. From the pulpit I gazed at the people; sixty or so were in attendance. With great excitement and exuberance, I began to relate the miracle-working power of God in my life as He saved me, filled me with His Spirit, and began to do the work of purifying His vessel for His service. I spoke with great enthusiasm for forty-five minutes or so.

After the meeting, I was greeted by several people who shook my hand and said, "God bless you, brother Don. Eventually you'll calm down. You'll settle down." One person said, "Praise the Lord, brother Don. I hope you find a nice church to settle down in and a good pastor to take care of you." Obviously, some of the folks weren't too thrilled with my presentation! Some even dozed through the meeting and weren't quite sure about what I said during the service. In spite of the lack of encouragement, I walked away from that meeting determined that I would not settle down, quiet down, or become one who would just fit into the mold of average Christianity. Even at that young age I was very fearful that being the average Christian would mean missing most of what God had for me in life. My greatest fear in life is to be on my deathbed knowing that I have not accomplished that for which I was born. The cry of my heart is to accomplish all that is on God's heart for me to do in this life.

As time and the will of the Lord would have it, ten years later I found myself invited back to that same little church for another Sunday evening meeting. With great excitement and anticipation, I entered the pulpit. When I looked over the people, an amazing sight greeted me. The same 60 folks were scattered in their same seats throughout the church. They had the same expressions on their faces, and some may have even had on the same clothes! At any rate, not much had changed during the previous decade.

I greeted the people and said, "Well, friends, here I am. Ten years later, almost to the day. And I have not calmed down, and I have not cooled off. If anything, I am more on fire, more radically committed, more sold out to God's purposes. I believe I hear His voice more clearly now than I ever have in my life. And it's only by His grace that I can stand up here and say that to you."

He wants us to grow in grace, to grow in knowledge, intimacy, and fellowship with the Lord Jesus so that we will have greater zeal and steadfastness of commitment to Him with each passing day. The more we say yes to Him, the more we experience the acceleration of spiritual growth. The softer your heart is before God, the greater the acceleration of His will becomes in your life. When we are soft before Him, we are prime candidates for His Manifest Presence.

> THE MORE WE SAY "YES" TO HIM, THE MORE WE EXPERIENCE THE ACCELERATION OF SPIRITUAL GROWTH.

God wants what He is doing in each individual heart to be accelerated. He wants an acceleration of His will in our lives. It is important to note, however, that this acceleration comes from Him; it cannot be produced in the flesh. When our foot presses the accelerator of a car, the engine takes over and the vehicle's speed increases. Similarly, when we respond to God by opening our hearts, His power takes over, propelling us in the direction of greater spiritual growth.

As we are able to respond to Him and willing to respond to Him, we will experience that acceleration. Joel says, "Tearing your clothes is not enough to show that you are sad. Let your hearts be broken..." (Joel 2:13). In the Old Testament, the sign that somebody was totally, emotionally repentant or totally, emotionally appalled was that the individual would rip his or her clothes. When David found out that his son was sick, for example, the Bible says that David fasted and lay on the ground for seven days (2 Sam. 12:16-17 NASB).

That was the sign of his utter grief over his son's death.

In the Book of Acts we read that the people of Lystra called Paul a god and they were ready to burn incense to him. Paul's response was to go out in the middle of the streets and tear his clothes (see Acts 14:11-16). In effect, he was saying, "I am totally appalled that you would mistake me for a god." It was a violent gesture he used to get their attention.

The prophet Joel, however, could see right through the outward act. When people tear their clothes it is an outward demonstration, but it does not necessarily require things to change on the inside. Joel said, "I'll tell you what, guys. Stop tearing your clothes, and start tearing your heart. Stop just pretending you've repented, and really repent. Stop pretending you're serving God, and start to serve Him with a pure heart." (See Joel 2:13.)

You can serve the Lord without serving Him from the sanctuary or without serving Him from a pure heart. This happens when you serve Him out of a sense of obligation or fear or guilt. It happens if you serve Him for personal gain or personal popularity. All that kind of service is external and fleshly. It's like tearing the clothes, but it's not tearing the heart.

God wants people who will tear their hearts, not their clothes. He wants people who will serve Him from the depths of their hearts. Such folks will purify their hearts "and makes himself pure like Christ" (1 John 3:3). Job said, "Look, though God may kill me, yet I will trust in Him" (Job 13:15). We think, "Oh, God's going to do such great things for me. I'm going to serve Him. If I serve God, He'll buy me a car. If I serve God, He'll let me become a big rock star. If I serve God, He'll make me into a big evangelist who will go around the world and preach to millions of people. If I serve God, He'll prosper my publishing company." That kind of motivation stinks; it is a literal stench in the nostrils of God.

> GOD WANTS PEOPLE WHO WILL TEAR THEIR HEARTS, NOT THEIR CLOTHES.

Job said, "I'll tell you what, God. You can slay me, and I'll still praise you" (see Job 13:15). Do you remember the three Hebrew children? Nebuchadnezzar said to them, "Either you deny God, or I will throw you into the fiery furnace."

The boys answered, "We will not deny our God. God can deliver us from a fiery furnace." And just before they went in, Shadrach, Meshach, and Abednego added, "Oh, by the way, King Nebuchadnezzar, even if He doesn't deliver us, we still wouldn't bow to your god. Even if we walk in there and we get burned to a crisp, we still wouldn't serve your god" (Dan. 3:15-18—author's paraphrase).

Job had lost his children, his land, and his cattle. He had lost everything. Dogs were licking his sores, and he said, "Lord, though you slay me, yet will I praise you." This is ministry from the sanctuary. (See Job 1-2.) Yet some of us have trouble serving God when everything is going right, let alone when things go wrong.

"Listen, I stand at the door. I am knocking" (Revelation 3:20).

This is a great salvation Scripture. We use it in evangelism all the time. But the Lord is knocking on the doors of Christian hearts, too. He is saying, "Let me in. Let me in the door of your heart."

At a motel where I recently stayed, I noticed there were three locks on the door of the room. Just before getting into bed, I went over to lock the door. I thought I would merely push the button on one of the locks instead of securing all three. But then I realized, "No, if they've got three locks on the door, it's probably because I should use them."

We may be that way with God. We put all kinds of locks on the doors, but He keeps on knocking.

We may respond, "But, Lord, how about this other room? It's all ready for you."

"No, I want to come in this room," He insists.

He is coming and will thoroughly purge His threshing floor (see Matt. 3:12). He will "burn the chaff" and clean it up so He can come and establish Himself there. He wants us to come into a place of maturity so that we will be able to give an accurate representation of Heaven here on earth. Can you imagine God's disgust at everything that goes on in His name? It scares me to think about it. Our prayer should be, "Lord, what can I do in your name that will be an accurate representation of what you're doing in Heaven?"

When I do something in the name of Jesus, in effect, I'm saying, "If Jesus were here, He'd be doing the same thing." When I say, "In Jesus' name," I'm saying Jesus would do the same thing. But would He? Would He be doing those things? It's the same principle He used when He said that He never did anything unless He saw His Father in Heaven doing it (see John 8:28). Whatever He saw His Father in Heaven doing, that's what He did.

24-Hour Purity

Look at the kind of love that the Father has given us: We are called children of God. And, we really are God's children! The people in the world don't understand it, because they have not known Him. Dear friends, we are not children of God. It does not yet appear what we will be in the future. We know when Christ comes again, we will be like him. We will see him as He really is. Christ is pure and every person who has this hope based on Christ makes himself pure like Christ (1 John 3:1-3).

In a similar vein, Matthew wrote, "People who have pure hearts are happy because they will see God" (Matt. 5:8). Do you want to see the Lord? John said, "Anyone who has this hope [the hope of seeing the Lord Jesus] purifies himself, even as He is pure." Who wants to see God? It continues to be a matter of heart, doesn't it? A *pure* heart because my heart is His sanctuary. Whenever I am ministering from my heart, from the love, from the compassion, from the joy, from the desire that God put within me, I am beginning to minister from His fullness. And when my heart is pure and there's no brackishness there, then His life is free to flow through me. I can let loose and move with His passion.

Brackishness and impurity block the flow of God's anointing. They tarnish the purity of God's words through us. Our perspective is biased and our motives are weak when we don't minister from purity.

We often say, "God, give me your fullness," but we've got our hands full of other things. "God, fill my heart with Yourself," and our hearts are so cluttered that He can't even find a place to sit. It's like our house on Christmas morning. There's no place to sit. There are too many toys and too much wrapping paper lying around. Yet, for those of us who want to see the Lord, who will purify ourselves, who will make a place within our hearts for Him to come in, there will be room for the Lord to rule and minister.

> WE OFTEN SAY, "GOD, GIVE ME YOUR FULL-NESS," BUT WE'VE GOT OUR HANDS FULL OF OTHER THINGS.

The Lord once said to me, *"You know how you can tell when you're being religious?"*

"How?" I asked.

"When you treat your wife differently than you treat people in the church, you're being religious. Your wife and your children deserve the same treatment you give to a church member. Your family deserves the same compassion, the same love, the same understanding, the same mercy."

He showed me that if I don't treat Cathy with the same degree of patience I have for a church member, then I'm in sin. I can't say, "Lord, I'm just too tired; she has to be there for me." If that is my attitude, I have to repent. It's a matter of heart. It begins in *my* heart. The extension of my heart is my home. The extension of my home is the church. The extension of the church is the community, then the state, then the country, and the world. But it starts in my heart. How I treat the Lord, then, is how I treat my spouse, my sons, and my friends.

Sometimes I lament, "Lord, you know I just get so angry sometimes. Please help me." Whenever I get angry with my boys and I know it's an unrighteous anger, I get under such conviction that I have to humble myself and go to them. I have to ask them to forgive me. "Daddy was wrong. Daddy sinned. I had to go to Jesus and ask Him to forgive me. I shouldn't have treated you that way. Will you forgive me?"

It's not easy to do this. Who likes to go to a nine-year-old and tell him you've sinned against him? One of my youngest sons has said at such a time, "You sinned. You didn't make Jesus happy, Dad." Following such a confession, I hear about it for two days from my five-year-old son, Joel. But that's good for me because the issue is honesty. The real question is, Do I want to see God? If my answer is yes, I will purify myself. I will purify my heart, my relationships with my wife and my children, and all my relationships so that I can see God.

> *The Lord is not slow to keep His promise. No, He is patient with you. He wants everyone to find room for a change in their hearts. He doesn't want anyone to be lost. The Day of the Lord will come suddenly, like a robber. The heavens will pass away with a whizzing noise. The elements will be destroyed with heat. The earth and every force in it will be gone* (2 Peter 3:9-10).

What kind of people should we be? Obviously, God has called us to be people of holiness, people of right conduct. Only as such can we hasten the day of the Lord. Only then can there be an acceleration of God's will for us. It's so easy to be offended, so easy to quit, so easy to give up. We could say, "I've had enough of this." But a desire to enter into His fullness (everything that God has for us) pushes us to go on. We must allow God to have His way, to allow Him to do His work within.

I don't think we can ever become too spiritual. When we become spiritual we become like Enoch, who walked with God and "was not" (see Gen. 5:24). He was just translated. Until we are translated, we can be as spiritual as we need to be. The requirements the Holy Spirit puts on us are not beyond our ability. We need to be soft and flexible and allow the purity of the Lord to flow through us. We are called to be people who can minister from our hearts.

If our hearts are hard or angry or bitter or hurt, we cannot minister from the sanctuary because those things close us off from a place of purity within. God wants us to minister in purity from the sanctuary of our hearts, whether it's to an individual or through preaching, or if it's officiating at marriages or pastoring people or prophesying or whatever it is we're doing. There is a deeper relationship with God that we can experience if we open our hearts to His Manifest Presence.

God is coming to this earth. It's going to happen. We're already experiencing it to a degree. Ministries are seeing God move in unpredictable ways. When you pay the price, God moves. I'm not content just to read about it or hear about it. I'm not even content to publish it or to write it. I want to experience it. I want to see the Lord.

WHEN YOU PAY THE PRICE, GOD MOVES.

When we learn to minister in purity from the sanctuary of our hearts, God's Manifest Presence will move in our midst. As Watchman Nee pointed out, that's "the normal Christian life."[1] The time is coming when the Lord in His fullness will so motivate us that we will not want to leave His house. What a day of rejoicing that will be! That is His promise for us in this life. If we are willing and obedient, we will eat the good of the land and experience His fullness.

ENDNOTE

1. Watchman Nee, *The Normal Christian Life* (Carol Stream, Illinois: Tyndale House Publishers, 1977).

Presence Ponderings

1. As a flashlight illuminates a darkened room, so does the flow of the Spirit illuminate our spiritual vision and understanding.

2. Carnal religiosity promotes hypocritical behavior. God's Presence and power dwell in the hearts of those who love Him enough to obey Him even when no one is watching.

3. With the same diligence that we tend to our gardens in the natural, we must likewise take time to discard of the weeds that choke our spiritual lives.

4. When you serve the Lord with ulterior motives, it's like the outward act of tearing the clothes without tearing the heart.

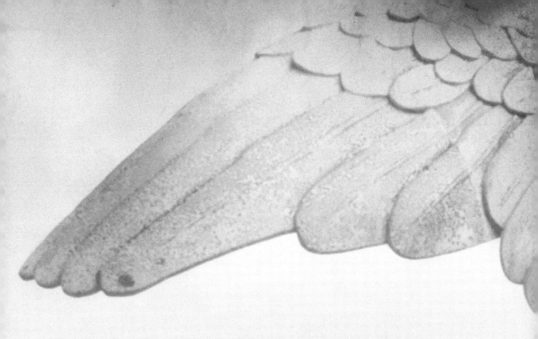

CHAPTER 4

God's Plan—His Word Within

The Real Power of God's Word in Us

The Always-Present One looks into a person's feelings. He searches through a person's thoughts (Proverbs 20:27).

The Word of God turns on this lamp: "Your words enlighten, instructing the simple-minded ones" (Ps. 119:130). The Word becomes "Your word [is like] a lamp for my feet, and a light for my path" (Ps. 119:105), and we are responsible for walking in the light that is revealed to us—the light of truth, wisdom, and honesty.

Whenever the Word of God is revealed or whenever it is spoken, it "turns the light on" in our understanding. When I was first saved, I came to the Lord with many hang-ups, not the least of which was the fact that I was afraid of the dark. Here I was, a nineteen-year-old sophomore in college, needing to sleep with a light on in my dormitory room. This may seem ridiculous to you, but fear of the dark was a real phobia for me.

After I was born again, I began to read the Word, and I came upon the Scripture that says, "Perfect love casts out fear" (1 John 4:18 NASB). When I saw that truth, I decided to embrace it and I said, "Thank you,

Lord Jesus, 'Perfect love does cast out fear.' I never have to be afraid again." After that time of prayer, I would go into my dormitory room at night, get ready for bed, shut off the light and jump into bed, but I would still shake in my sheets with fear. I began to repeat, "'Perfect love casts out fear.' God, I love you perfectly. I love you perfectly. I love you perfectly." After two or three nights of that repetitious approach not working, I began to wonder just how valid the Word of God was. Prior to this, from the time when I was born again, I had enjoyed the experience of the Word of God working in my life. What the Word said, happened in my experience. I began to wonder what was going wrong.

As I opened the Scriptures again I asked God to help me understand the meaning of the verse: "Perfect love casts out fear" (1 John 4:18 NASB). I began to realize that I could not love God perfectly, but that *He loved me perfectly*. I had the concept backward. Fear ends, not when I love God perfectly (because I am incapable of such love), but fear loses its dominion over me when I appropriate the truth that God, in fact, loves me perfectly. From that time on, I did not fear the dark.

> I BEGAN TO REALIZE THAT I COULD NOT LOVE GOD PERFECTLY, BUT THAT *HE LOVED ME PERFECTLY.*

When the Word of the Lord comes into a person's heart, and the light turns on, we see the Word for what it really is, and it changes us.

One summer afternoon, my second oldest son, Donald, got into the paints in my workshop, in spite of the fact that he knew full well that he was not permitted to use them. He stained one of his nicer shirts with green enamel. He quickly took his shirt off, put it into the clothes hamper, and dressed in another shirt.

Later in the afternoon, I noticed he had changed clothes and I asked him, "Donald, why do you have a different shirt on?"

He replied, "Oh, the other one got dirty, and I wanted to be clean, so I put a clean shirt on."

"Oh, okay," I responded.

It didn't take more than about a day for his mom to discover the shirt in the wash, at which time Donald was summoned into the kitchen. When he was presented with the evidence of what he had done, he had to give an explanation for the splotches of green enamel on his shirt. He finally got around to explaining the incident by telling us how he had sneaked into the workshop to get some paint for his tree house and spilled some of the paint on his shirt.

I confronted him with, "Well, why did you lie to me when I asked you why you changed your shirt?"

"Well, I did get it dirty, but I was hoping that if I just threw it in with the dirty clothes, it would get washed, and no one would ever know it." My oldest son, Jonathan, who was in the process of just beginning his memory verses at school, was listening to this conversation. All of a sudden he got an amazing gleam in his eye and a big smile on his face as he recited the following verse: "Be sure your sin will find you out" (Num. 32:23 KJV). He went on, "Now I know what that means. When you do something wrong and try to hide it, it will come out anyway." We all had a good laugh as we saw the Holy Spirit's light shining in our oldest son's heart, realizing he was learning in a new way what the Scriptures meant. The insight shared by Jonathan helped Donald to see his need as well.

What we see when "the light comes on" is what we need to deal with in our lives. When the Word of God is spoken, the lamp of the Lord turns on within our spirits and we know what the Lord expects of us.

The "flashlight principle" comes into play here again. Covered by the blood of Jesus, we can walk into the full light of God's Presence, without fear of what the full light will discover. Whatever shows up, our softness of heart and our confidence in the Lord Jesus causes us to quickly deal with the sin.

A father may say to his teen-aged son, "Clean up the garage." Somewhat lacking in zeal, the son will go into the garage. There he may encounter darkness, and won't even know where to begin until he turns on the light. (Actually, he would like to avoid the light for fear of what it may reveal!) When he finally turns the light on, he discovers what needs to be done. He is accountable to his father for straightening up the mess. He is compelled to begin his work.

In the same way, when the lamp of the Lord comes on, we know what we are supposed to do. God wants us to be people who are not just *hearers* of the Word, but *doers* of the Word (see James 1:22). When the Word of God shines its unavoidable light in particular areas of our lives, we know what we have to do. In order to experience a truth that is revealed to us, in order to walk in that truth, we are required to see ourselves in the light of God's Word. If we want to minister in the fullness of God's light, we must first let this light do its work within us. The Lord wants us to walk in truth, not just talk about it, not just sing about it, not just dance about it, but *walk* in truth. He wants us to become what the Word is saying.

> IF WE WANT TO MINISTER IN THE FULLNESS OF GOD'S LIGHT, WE MUST FIRST LET THIS LIGHT DO ITS WORK WITHIN US.

The world is full of people who have their doctrine straight. That's good. The Church is full of people who "know" what the Word is saying and "know" what the Word requires. That's important. There are many experts, many theologians, many individuals with great understanding of the things revealed by the Word of God. The problem is that the world is grossly lacking in people who are actually experiencing what they say they believe.

When the world begins to be filled with Christians who are experiencing what they believe, then you will see the nations standing up and taking notice. I have made a personal commitment to the Lord that my heart and my passion will be to be a doer of the Word, not just to have the ability to explain deep and mighty doctrines, not merely to explore theoretically the deep recesses of the spiritual realm, but that the passion of my life will be to *experience* the deep things of God. I want to touch God and fellowship with Him and experience Him. I love Him. That love compels me to experience Him.

The apostle John declares, "About the Message of life: What has existed since the beginning we heard, we saw with our own eyes, we watched, we touched with our hands. Now to you also we are telling the things we have seen and heard…" (1 John 1:1,3). The things I teach and preach are truths of the Word of God that I am experiencing now or anticipate being able to experience in the near future. I want my life to be the living Word of God in experience so that when the world sees me, I won't have to convince them with my words that what I am saying is true. I want my life to demonstrate the truth of what I believe. It is people who live in that manner who will change the world.

The Bible says that "the Word became human and lived among us" (John 1:14). That Word was spoken eons ago. God still wants His Word to become flesh in you and me. This is how the world will know that He truly is the Lord. Admittedly, sometimes when the light comes on, it's too bright for us. It hurts. Sometimes the light turns on, and we see things we don't want to see. What the light reveals makes us angry. We even get angry at God. We get angry at the Word because we see things we don't like. It scares us, and so we want to reject and avoid what God is saying to us.

There are not too many of us who would have to look too deeply into our lives to find places where God's Word continually tries to bring light to us. Yet, for one reason or another, we are able to explain away or otherwise postpone the inevitable—God's having His way in our lives. Our progress is hindered and our walk with God is stifled because when His Word brings light we do not respond to it.

Getting on the Cutting Edge

To be on the cutting edge of God's plan for this hour is to be on the cutting edge of the Spirit and His work in our personal lives. Whenever you and I see areas of our lives enlightened by God's Word, and we truly want to be on the cutting edge, we must not attempt to explain away, justify, or rationalize that which we see wrong in our lives. We must not transfer responsibility to someone else. Our calling is to be people who simply say yes to the Lord, find a place of heartfelt repentance, and ask for His forgiveness and His anointing to overcome that particular weakness or sin. Then, we can continue on with full, innocent, unabated fellowship with the Lord. The process of maturing is the ability to have the light shine in our hearts, and instead of running from that light, to submit to it and repent.

> THE PROCESS OF MATURING IS THE ABILITY TO HAVE THE LIGHT SHINE IN OUR HEARTS, AND INSTEAD OF RUNNING FROM THAT LIGHT, TO SUBMIT TO IT AND REPENT.

Those who love sin dwell in darkness. John dealt very clearly with this in his first letter. But when the light shines in their hearts, those who love light embrace the light and repent of what the light reveals so that they can continue to live in purity. We are on the cutting edge of His purposes when the Holy Spirit is given full access to be on the cutting edge of our flesh-life. Maturing people do not reject the light of the Holy Spirit as He shines His Word in their hearts, correcting them, rebuking them, changing them and causing them to adjust their thoughts and actions to conform more to the image and likeness of Jesus Christ.

We know we are maturing when God can put the light on in a particular area of our lives and our response is to want to deal with it and to do all we can to obey the Lord. We can let His light shine as brightly as He wants it to shine, and we can respond by growing up without grumbling against the Lord, grumbling against the Bible or deciding we don't want to read the Word anymore because it tells us things we don't want to hear. The process of growing up demands that the more you grow up, the less complaining you will do. The more you mature, the less hassle you'll give the Holy Ghost.

Paul says, "Do not frustrate the grace of God" (Gal. 2:21 KJV). You can frustrate God's grace by not doing according to the Word that is shining upon you and within you. God wants us to be people who are responding to the light.

"Your words enlighten" (Ps. 119:130). And when that light shines, grown-up Christians (or growing-up Christians) are those who can respond to the light. We know what to do simply because the light is shining. Maturing people are making way for His Manifest Presence.

This process is important because we are on a journey in life. Our journey is based on the purposes of God. We are on a journey to discover and fulfill God's plan for this generation. We are on a journey in which God wants us to experience what He has planned for us in the process of the restoration of His Church. As the Word of God shines upon us, we are required to walk in truth and to walk in light. Every step God requires us to take causes us to change for the good. God's Word comes forth so that we can change and mature. God's Word comes forth so that we will grow up, so that as mature sons we can carry out His purposes. God has always wanted a dwelling place. He's always wanted a house. He's always wanted a people for His own possession. We can become that dwelling place only as we mature as sons of God.

It's one thing to have some exciting revelation from the Word of God, but it's another thing to apply that revelation to our lives in such a way that it works. As stated earlier, one of the gravest errors in Christendom involves the accumulating of knowledge of the Word for the sake of knowledge, without accumulating the Word for the sake of our personal lives.

The goal is for me to *become* the Word, so I can walk in the Word, and in the truth. I am not interested in just *knowing* the Word. I am interested in becoming that which God wants me to be. It is not the *hearers* who are justified, it is the *doers* who are justified. The doers who become the Word of God personified in this world are the people in whom God seeks to establish His dwelling place as it is typified in Solomon's Temple.

> THE GOAL IS FOR ME TO *BECOME* THE WORD, SO I CAN WALK IN THE WORD, AND IN THE TRUTH.

God Has Chosen Zion

"The Always-Present One has chosen Jerusalem. He wants it for

His home" (Ps. 132:13). The Lord further declares, "This is my resting-place forever. Here is where I want to stay, (Ps. 132:14). Zion is a type of the Church, so when God says, "The Lord has chosen Zion, He has desired it for His habitation," He is declaring that He has chosen us for His resting place, His dwelling place, His habitation.

He could come to my home and say, "For the Lord has chosen this property; He has desired it for His home," meaning that He will move in and live there. He could do this, but we know God doesn't choose brick and mortar to accomplish His purposes; He chooses you and me. He says Zion is, "…my resting-place forever. Here is where I want to stay. I will bless her (the city of Jerusalem) with plenty of nourishment. I will satisfy her poor people with food. I will let her priests receive deliverance. And, those of her who follow God will truly sing for joy!" (Ps. 132:14-16).

God will take up a permanent dwelling place in the Church. At the end of Hebrews 9, we find an interesting Scripture. It says that Jesus appeared once to bear sin, and that He will appear a second time, not as our Sin-bearer, but as the Bearer of Salvation (Heb. 9:27). As long as Jesus is our Sin-bearer, as long as we persist with the false theology that we all sin every day and constantly are falling short of what God wants us to do, then we cannot experience Jesus, the Manifester of salvation in our lives.

This is merely an excuse for not living a holy life. Certainly we need the grace of God, and certainly we cannot succeed without His grace, and certainly the only way we can get through a day without gross sin is by allowing God to have His way in us. He is living His life through me. But as long as we willfully and persistently sin and then go to the Lord Jesus for repentance, Jesus remains to us a Sin-bearer, but never the Bearer of the fullness of Salvation.

The Bible promises us that Jesus wants to be more than just our Sin-bearer; He wants to be to us all that salvation is meant to be. As Isaiah 53:5 says, "But he was wounded for the things that *we* did wrong. He was crushed for the evil things *we* did. The punishment, which made us well, was given to *Him*. And, we are healed because of *His* wounds."

In that one verse we find the entire redemption of humankind: body, soul, and spirit. Jesus wants to manifest His full salvation to us and not just provide redemption from sin. If you and I are the Church, this means He wants to take up His permanent dwelling place in you and me. This will enable Him to have His fullest expression through us. He won't use a lectern. He won't use a guitar. He won't use a satellite dish. His glory will dwell in flesh and blood, in people who call upon the name of the Lord and allow Him to have His perfect expression through them individually!

Jesus has never wanted to come just to visit. He has always wanted to come to stay, to dwell permanently so that revival would be an intense, continual experience of His Presence that grows greater and greater and greater. For Him to take up permanent residence in my life, in my fellowship, in my ministry, in my town, means His Lordship ruling and reigning over me and over all that He has given me to care for. That means a radical alteration of my plans, a radical alteration of how I conduct my business, because Jesus has come to stay. And when He comes to stay, everything changes—permanently.

In the last days, this is what is going to happen: The hill upon which the Always-Present One's temple stands will become the most important of all hills. It will be raised above the other hills. Various peoples will flow to it. Many nations will come and say: "Come, let us go up to the mountain of the Always-Present One, and to the temple of the God of Jacob! Then God will teach us from His ways. And, we will live by His paths." His teachings will go forth from Zion. The mes-

sage of the Always-Present One will go out from Jerusalem (Micah 4:1-2).

The prophets saw Zion as the central focus of God's glory to be spread throughout the earth. Micah pointed out that many nations will come to its light, and many will say, "Come, let us go up to the mountain of the Lord, let us go up to Mount Zion, that He may teach us about His ways, so that we may walk in His paths. For out of Zion [out of the Church] the law will go forth, and the word of the Lord will go forth from Jerusalem."

In a very serious, as well as exciting way, we realize that God's Presence, God's power, God's anointing, and God's glory will flow forth from the Church (out of Zion). "His teachings will go forth from Zion" (Mic. 4:2). The law, the law of Christ, is the law of liberty. It is not the law of rules and regulations, but it is the law of liberty. Out of Zion shall go forth the good news, the law of liberty that declares you are *free* from sin, *free* from the bondage of self, *free* from fears, *free* from hassles, *free* from the things that happened to you as a child, free indeed! This is beginning to occur even now as God is manifesting His Presence among us.

> *At that time, people will no longer say: "The fathers have eaten sour grapes. And that caused the children to grind their teeth from the sour taste." But each person will die for his own sin. The person who eats sour grapes will grind his own teeth* (Jeremiah 31:29-30).

No longer are the sins and iniquities of our ancestors to rule over us. Our wholeness was purchased at Calvary by the blood of Jesus Christ. We are no longer subject to the brokenness of our childhood or our pre-Christ lives. Those chains are once and for all broken. The law of liberty declares that in Christ *you are free*. That is the good news that will be proclaimed from Mount Zion, the Church. The only reason good news can come forth out of Zion is because Someone is dwelling there. That Someone is God, who has chosen Zion to be His dwelling place. When God is dwelling in Zion, His Word is going forth.

Zion—The Place of God's Fullness

Out of Zion (the Church) all that God wants to be fulfilled will happen. It will happen to those and through those who dwell in Zion because that's where God is. Zion is really the place of fullness. When we talk about the fullness of God, we are describing His completion, His wholeness in us. The fullness of God goes forth from *Zion*, the *Church*. Jesus is "a minister in the most holy place, the tent which is real. God, not man, put up this tent" (Heb. 8:2).

In Hebrews 9:11 we see another important truth, "But when Christ appeared as a high priest of the good things to come, He entered through the greater and more perfect tabernacle, not made with hands, that is to say, not of this creation...." Jesus is the One who ministers from the sanctuary, from the very throne room of God. And when God dwells within us, that is where His throne room is. Jesus wants to minister from God's throne room (within us) in all of His fullness and power and with the freedom of expression to be all He wants to be through you and me.

God wants His Tabernacle to be among humankind. The Scriptures say, "God's sanctuary is among human beings" (see Rev. 21:3). The word *Emmanuel* means "God with us." His intention was never to communicate to us from afar, but to dwell in our hearts from a place of permanent intimacy. "The Always-Present One has chosen Jerusalem. He wants it for His home" (Ps. 132:13). He wants to live there *perpetually*. What excitement there is in knowing that God's permanent residence is inside you and me. His permanent residence is in the

Church. When God comes in, everything He is and everything He has, comes with Him. That requires everything that is out of harmony with God to change.

> HIS INTENTION WAS NEVER TO COMMUNI-
> CATE TO US FROM AFAR, BUT TO DWELL IN
> OUR HEARTS FROM A PLACE OF PERMANENT
> INTIMACY.

An examination of the gospels clearly illustrates this. Every time Jesus entered a situation, things happened. Some people were made glad; some were made angry; some were healed; demons were cast out; words of knowledge and revelation were given and visions were seen. Jesus manifested the glory and the fullness of God wherever He went. Where He was and where He walked, everything and everyone came under divine order, or else they fled. When God's Presence is manifested in the Church, all things come under divine order. First, His presence brings us into divine order as individuals, and then that which is around us falls into divine order as the Manifest Presence of God moves among us.

If you invite me to your home for an evening of fellowship, I don't leave half my intellect or half my personality or half my body somewhere else. When I come to visit you, everything I am comes with me—my mind, my body, my emotions, my spirit! You get my beard, my voice, my sense of humor, and my feet! You get me in all my fullness. You get my full frame—all six feet, two inches of me! Similarly, when God comes to dwell in His Church, He comes in all His fullness. The Scriptures say, "it pleased God to have the totality live in Christ" (Col. 1:19). It is the Father's good pleasure for all His fullness to dwell in the Lord Jesus. Paul says, "that you will be filled with the totality of God" (Eph. 3:19). It is the Father's good pleasure *for us* to be filled with all the fullness of God. If we are to be filled with all the fullness of God, we need to understand that everything God is, He wants to give to us.

There is a place of fullness, a place of fulfillment in God where everything He is will be expressed in the Church.

> *What about this salvation? The prophets spoke about this gracious love which was meant for you. They searched very carefully for the time and the way that things would happen. The Spirit of Christ was in them, showing them. Long ago, they told the truth about the sufferings of Christ and the glories that came later. It was revealed to them that they were serving you, not themselves! Now, men who preach the Good News have told you these things by the Holy Spirit who was sent from heaven. Even angels want to bend down to look into these things (1 Peter 1:10-12).*

The prophets of old were men who could understand the significance of what they were seeing and saying. They were men who could see beyond themselves and into eternity. Joel was not primarily concerned with locusts and seasonal rains; he saw something beyond his own time and space. He saw something for us. Isaiah did not have a primary interest in pottery. God was speaking to him about things of eternal value. Jesus' ultimate concern was not for lilies, birds, or Solomon's glory. He was speaking to us, transcending time and space with a view toward eternal principles that would forever change humankind's concept of God.

The Lord is again looking for a people who will follow His ways. His Spirit is brooding over the earth, seeking those who will break out of their own time and space and see the eternal significance of their relationship with Jesus. We are not here by accident. We are not saved by chance, but there is an eternal destiny that many, if not most of us, never enter. We are so filled with the needs of the moment, with the chores of making this life comfortable and our churches secure, that we cannot break through to see the significance of our destiny in life, to fulfill that for which we were born, to accomplish all that is on the Father's heart for our generation. Wilderness life has become so comfortable that we have forgotten that there is a Promised Land waiting to be possessed in this life.

> HIS SPIRIT IS BROODING OVER THE EARTH, SEEKING THOSE WHO WILL BREAK OUT OF THEIR OWN TIME AND SPACE AND SEE THE ETERNAL SIGNIFICANCE OF THEIR RELATIONSHIP WITH JESUS.

Many are excited about a new outpouring of the Holy Spirit. It will be glorious! Jesus is coming to stay! He is coming with light and love and power and revelation. But He is also coming to shake us out of our lethargy and complacency. Remember, great revival usually comes with great calamity.

Many of us remember the glorious manifestation of God's Presence in the late 1960s and early 1970s.

That period of time in church history is called the Charismatic Renewal. Millions were swept into the Kingdom during that wonderful time of seeing miracle after miracle after miracle.

But we must also remember what was taking place in the United States during that time. We were being ripped apart as a nation by terrible race riots. Three national leaders were assassinated. The Vietnam War was dividing us, and the oil crisis was crippling us. Our young people were discovering new and more deadly drugs to sniff or smoke or inject. Difficult times had truly come, and they drove us directly to Jesus.

Tough times cause us to seek God. They compel us to repent and do the will of God. We expect a major manifestation of God's Presence and masses of people coming to Jesus, but we must remember it will come with great calamity. God is coming to dwell among His people.

> WE EXPECT A MAJOR MANIFESTATION OF GOD'S PRESENCE AND MASSES OF PEOPLE COMING TO JESUS, BUT WE MUST REMEMBER IT WILL COME WITH GREAT CALAMITY.

He is coming to break us out of the confines of our ties to this earth with all its rusting and broken promises. When Jesus taught the disciples to pray, His prayer was simple: "May Your Kingdom come..." (Matt. 6:10). He didn't ask His Father for a convention center, a big ministry, or a Bible school. He didn't even ask for a newspaper or a publisher. His view was eternal. So should ours be.

Breaking Through Time and Space

When I think of the puny things I fret about every day, it causes me to repent before the Lord. We have a greater responsibility and a greater significance than most can see. We have established our careers, built our houses, put our finances in order, sent our children to Christian schools, stabilized our churches. Our little "spheres" and "streams" are established and all is well with middle-class "Christian" America. Or is it? Are we really fulfilling our destiny? Is all our activity in accord with what is on God's heart for us?

All of these things are essential; they are foundational to the work and mission of the Church, but they aren't the goals. They are the foundation on which the Church may go forth and do the work of the ministry. Stable families, good careers, controlled finances, and loving churches are beautiful expressions of the life of Jesus, but we should be using these as a platform to break beyond our own time and space.

God wants us to look beyond the puniness of our own whining desires and selfish prayers. He wants us to break through time and space by the power of the Holy Ghost. He wants us to transcend the limitations of our finite minds to fulfill that for which we were born. We must remember that we were born with destiny.

Some of you may remember the recent orange juice advertising campaign that stated simply, "O.J.—it isn't just for breakfast anymore!" To tackle the "breakfast stigma" of orange juice seems to be no easy task! It has been a fixture on the morning table ever since man first squeezed the orange. To break with that mindset must have been a monumental task, but for the industry to grow, the breakfast attitude had to be broken.

God wants to change our mindsets about Him as well. The Holy Spirit spoke to me clearly one Sunday morning recently. He said, *"I'm not just for Sundays any more."* I knew immediately that He was making an emphatic point by saying "any more," as though there was a time when He was just for Sundays. *"As a matter of fact,"* the Holy Spirit went on, *"I'm not just for Christians any more, either. I'm not just for revival. I'm not here just to vindicate your doctrine with a few miracles, or your 'stream' by a visitation."*

At the same time, the Scripture that many of us enjoy singing began to ring in my ears: "The Always-Present One is great, even *outside* the borders of Israel!" (Mal. 1:5). God is great and His Holy Spirit is alive and well *outside the Church*.

Jesus said, "…listen, I am telling you to look up and see the fields. They are ready for harvest now" (John 4:35). Of course! There is no harvest of hearts prepared unless the Holy Spirit goes out among sinners and blasphemers and prepares them to get saved. When we go, we go with the Holy Ghost, knowing that He's been there before, preparing the people for the implantation of the Word.

We need to begin to release our unbelief to the Lord and allow Him to have His way all the time, all around us. It's no big deal to have miracles in a church where there are several hundred believing people supporting and encouraging you to go on. But God is saying to us that it is time to dare to believe, dare to pray, dare to move out in the Spirit before the masses of sinners. Jesus' greatest supernatural displays were among the harlots and other heathen of the day. In fact, He experienced His greatest opposition to the miraculous and to His life inside the established church of the day.

God wants to display His greatness to a needy and dying world. He wants us to break out of ourselves and carry His Presence where the Holy Ghost already is preparing the harvest—to the masses.

We are entering a time of expectation. We hear people say, "I am expecting to be used of God at this time"; and "I am sensitive to the Holy Spirit to do whatever He wants me to do in whatever circumstances." I love the verse that says, "The wind blows wherever it wishes. You hear the sound of it, but you don't know where it comes from and where it is going. It is the same way with everyone who has been born from the Spirit" (John 3:8). To be born of the Spirit and be led by the Spirit is to break out of time and space and allow the Holy Ghost to blow us where He wants us.

As significant and central as the local church is, we must remember that the Church has its destiny because the individuals who make up the

Church have destiny. It is up to us to respond to Him, lest we take our place in history with other revivals that have gone before us and were satisfied with the old wine, "for it is good enough."

> AS SIGNIFICANT AND CENTRAL AS THE LOCAL CHURCH IS, WE MUST REMEMBER THAT THE CHURCH HAS ITS DESTINY BECAUSE THE INDIVIDUALS WHO MAKE UP THE CHURCH HAVE DESTINY.

"Christ appointed apostles, prophets, evangelists, spiritual shepherds, and teachers" (Eph. 4:11). The conclusion of this pericope says, "…Until we are all together. We must be united in our faith and knowledge of the Son of God. We must become like a full-grown man, reaching for the greatest potential of Christ (Eph. 4:13). The five-fold ministry (apostles, prophets, evangelists, pastors, and teachers) equips the Church to move in the fullness of God, being conformed to the image of Jesus Christ. It was never a stopping place, but a springboard by which all believers could come to maturity.

Everything God is, everything He has, all the power He possesses, He will express in the earth through you and me. He wants to bring you to a place of Solomon's Temple, or a place of fullness within your heart. But that place of fullness is bathed in blood, suffering, and sacrifice.

Presence Ponderings

1. To be on the cutting edge of God's plan is to allow God's inevitable plan to fully have its way in our lives.

2. To concede to the false doctrine that we all sin daily is to forfeit the full manifestation of God's saving grace and power in our lives.

3. God wants to break us out of our usual mindsets so that we are better equipped to carry His message to the masses.

4. Experiencing the empirical fullness of God is not without sacrifice, but is bathed in sacrificial blood of the Lamb.

Chapter 5

God's Type—Solomon's Temple

Brokenness

God is continually calling out those who are broken because it is these people who are able to carry His Presence to the world. He is calling out a remnant—those who are willing to pay the price to manifest the Presence of the Lord. It is the same call He issued to Abraham, Isaac, and Jacob.

The covenant was first made with Abraham.

*After these things, the message of the Always-Present One came to Abram in a vision. God said, "Don't be afraid, Abram. I am your Shield. Your reward will get bigger and bigger!" Abram said, "O Lord who is always present, what can You give me? I still have no children. Listen, since You have not given me a descendant, one of my slaves will be my heir. He is Eliezer, from the city of Damascus. Look, when I die, he will be the one who inherits everything I own!" But then the message of the Always-Present One came to Abram, saying, "Eliezer will **not** inherit your property. No, a real son, one who comes from your own body, will be your heir!" Then God took Abram outside and said, "Look up at the sky now and try to count the stars. Can you count them all?*

Of course not. Well, you will have just as many descendants as there are stars!" Abram believed the Always-Present One, and so the Always-Present One declared him to be a righteous man (Genesis 15:1-6).

God compares Abraham's descendants to the dust of the earth, to the sand of the seashore, to the stars of Heaven. And He says, "you will have just as many descendants as there are stars" (see Gen. 15:5). What a glory it is to be able to be called a descendant of Abraham. As we continue on, however, we see that it is not enough just to be a descendant of Abraham in order to be able to inherit the promises of God. Sarah didn't quite believe what God had said. Neither did Abraham. So they tried to produce many nations themselves.

In Genesis 16:15 we read that Hagar gave birth to a son, Ishmael, who was fathered by Abraham. Ishmael was blessed because he was Abraham's seed, but he did not have divine destiny on his life. It was not through Ishmael that the nations would be numbered. It was not through Ishmael that God's promise would take place. In Genesis 25 we see that Abraham took another wife and had more sons. They too were blessed, but neither were they the seed of promise.

Abraham's two best-known sons were Isaac and Ishmael. Both of these sons were blessed, but the seed of promise was carried by Isaac only. It wasn't enough to be the seed of Abraham. The only way was to be born of Isaac. "...your descendants will be declared in Isaac" (Gen. 21:12).

But God was still not done separating; for we find that Isaac also had two sons. Romans 9:13 gives us an abrupt description of God's perspective concerning these two sons: "I loved more than I loved Esau." The seed of promise would have to pass through Jacob. There, the pattern of separation was clearly established. God would not ultimately use *all* the seed of Abraham, nor would He be satisfied with *all* of Isaac's descendants. But the separation would be complete only through Jacob, whom God chose to love simply because He is God and can choose as He pleases.

The prophet Zechariah wrote that two-thirds of Abraham's descendants would be cut off, with only one-third left (see Zech. 13:8). The remnant will be made up of those He will "refine…as silver is purified, and test… as gold is tested" (Zech. 13:9). In Galatians 4 we see this same principle. It's not enough just to be Abraham's seed; it's not enough just to be born of Isaac. We need to be born of Abraham and of Isaac and of Jacob.

> *It is written that Abraham had two sons. The mother of one son was a slave woman. The mother of the other son was a free woman. Abraham's son from the slave woman was born in the normal human way, but the son from the free woman was born because of the promise which God made to Abraham. This true story is an example for us: The two women are like the two agreements between God and men. One agreement is the law which God made on Mount Sinai. The people who are under this agreement are like slaves. The mother, named Hagar, is like that agreement. So Hagar is like Mount Sinai in Arabia. She represents the city of Jerusalem today. This city is a slave, and all of its people are slaves to the law, but the heavenly Jerusalem which is above is like the free woman. This is our mother. It is written: "Be happy, O woman who cannot have children! You never gave birth. Shout and cry out with joy!... (Galatians 4:22-27).*

The birth of Ishmael presents us with a very interesting situation. Ishmael was born of the flesh, whereas Isaac was born of the promise. The Scriptures say, "So, Hagar gave birth to Abram's son. Abram named his son Ishmael. Hagar was the mother. Abram was 86 years old when Hagar gave birth to Ishmael for him" (Gen. 16:15-16). Thirteen years pass between Genesis 16 and 17. In the 17th chapter we read, "When Abram was 99 years old, the Always-Present One appeared to him…" (Gen. 17:1). Ishmael had lived in Abram's house for 13 years. He was in early adolescence, just entering puberty, and his father was 99 years old!

Can you imagine starting your family at the age of 86? Isaac had not even been born yet. The Scriptures say that Abraham was 100 years old when Isaac was born! Ishmael would have been 14 at the time of Isaac's birth. Even though Ishmael was born of the flesh, until Isaac came, Ishmael could live in his father's house. Ishmael lived there; he got his sustenance there; he was nurtured there; he grew up there. Abraham was his father. He lived in Abraham's house for 14 years.

But what happened after Isaac was born? Isaac was the son of the free woman, the son of promise. The Scriptures tell us many things about Isaac:

> *The child (Isaac) grew and was ready to be weaned. Abraham gave a big party on the day of Isaac's weaning. Sarah saw the son of Hagar making fun. Then Sarah said to Abraham, "Make this slave-woman and her son go away! The son of this slave-girl will **not** share the inheritance with my son, Isaac." This matter about Abraham's son, Ishmael, was a very bad situation for Abraham. However, God said to Abraham, "Don't be worried about the boy or your slave-woman. Do everything that Sarah says to you. Listen to her, because your descendants will be declared in Isaac. I will also make a nation from the son of this slave-woman, because he descends from you, too!" (Genesis 21:8-13)*

He would still make Ishmael a nation, but the descendants of Abraham would be named through Isaac.

We often talk about and reflect upon God's telling Abraham to take Isaac up to the mountain in order to sacrifice him, but we forget that God required something else of Abraham that must have been very difficult as well. God commanded Abraham to banish his 14-year-old son. "Throw out the slave woman and her son! The son of the free woman will receive everything that his father has, but the son of the slave woman will receive nothing" (Gal. 4:30). In Ishmael we see the type of our fleshly activities. God wants us to let that go in the same way He wanted Abraham to let the son of his flesh go.

God's promises and His purposes for us don't come as we stubbornly hold on to our fleshly activities and carnal ministries. Everything started in the flesh is doomed to produce death. People who carry God's Manifest Presence are those who are willing to discard the flesh as well as offer the spiritual to the Lord.

God told Abraham to cast out his son Ishmael and then commanded him to sacrifice Isaac! He believed God, but in the natural it looked pretty bleak. *Both* were apparently rejected by the Lord, but Abraham knew that God's plan was best. Even in his most critical test, Abraham chose to trust God rather than his own intellect.

PEOPLE WHO CARRY GOD'S MANIFEST PRESENCE ARE THOSE WHO ARE WILLING TO DISCARD THE FLESH AS WELL AS OFFER THE SPIRITUAL TO THE LORD.

We humans are a strange species indeed! We possess finite minds with finite reasoning abilities, and yet we are always trying to second-guess our infinite Lord who possesses infinite reasoning and wisdom.

Don't be afraid to cast out your Ishmael! Don't be afraid to offer your Isaac! Your utter abandonment to the Lord is pleasing to Him. Your child-like trust and devotion to Him is worship before the throne. The Bible says that those who trust Him will never be ashamed.

All the children were Abraham's seed, but they did not all carry the divine destiny. Not even all the sons of Isaac would carry the divine destiny upon their shoulders, fulfilling God's purposes. God spoke, and there was a people who would fulfill what God spoke. Not all of Abraham's seed fulfilled the promise; not all of Isaac's seed fulfilled God's destiny either. Even Isaac's chosen seed, Jacob, had to wrestle with the angel before he could receive the blessing.

There are two very important aspects of carrying the Ark, or experiencing the Manifest Presence of God, in an ongoing, on-growing way. They deal with our external life (what we show to others) and the life within. Our external life—our relationship to others, where we fellowship, how we fellowship, how we think, our attitudes, and our behavior—is an important part of us. But it is in the realm of the life within—how I allow God to deal with me that only God sees—that really counts. There's the self that everybody else sees, and then there's the self that only God sees. It's that second self that God wants to deal with.

It seems popular for folks today to talk about being on the cutting edge of what God is doing. It seems to be the latest catchword for Christians—the "cutting edge." If I am on the cutting edge of what God is doing in this hour, it's only because God is on the cutting edge of my heart. He is cutting me, penetrating through the hardness, getting inside that tremendous fortress of my heart that I've made sure no one else can see or get into.

It is infinitely preferable to be on the "cutting edge" rather than the dull edge of anything. So if I'm on the cutting edge of what God's doing in this hour, it means I have to let Him be on the cutting edge of my heart. He is making my mortal flesh a habitation where His Presence is pleased to dwell.

Let's imagine a man named Elmer Fleshful. He comes to the Lord, and after spending five years in church, he begins his ministry. Mr. Fleshful has been appointed to be Sunday school superintendent. He prays, "God, I will serve you. God, I'm going to be a minister for you. God, I'm going to do everything you want me to do." Elmer feels he has established his ministry; he is doing what God wants him to do. But before we see what happens to Elmer, let's go back to Ishmael and Isaac. Ishmael came before Isaac. Even though Ishmael was very dear to Abraham, and he was his son, an even greater son would appear. All of a sudden Isaac appeared, crying, "Make room for me!" Ishmael didn't want to leave home; his mother, Hagar, didn't want to go anywhere either, but there wasn't room for both Ishmael and Isaac in the same house.

Elmer Fleshful might say, "But, God, I'm a Sunday school superintendent; I'm doing your work!" God's response is, "Yes, but I want to move in that Sunday school. Isaac must come forth. The Ishmael of your flesh will have to go!"

This happens to each of us when we open ourselves to God's workmanship deep within. He cuts away at the flesh and reaches our spirit, from which He can truly work. Soon something new begins to be born in you, and you find yourself saying, "Man, I'm not comfortable any more. Something's wrong. My ministry's being challenged. What's happening? I used to be the greatest Sunday school superintendent this church ever had!"

The Isaac's coming. Come on, Elmer, make room for the Isaac. The only way the Isaac can take control is if we cast out the Ishmael. That which is born of the Spirit must displace all fleshly activity and ministry, no matter how good. "The son of the free woman will receive everything that his father has, but the son of the slave woman will receive nothing" (Gal. 4:30).

If we're to be on the cutting edge of what God is doing in this hour, if we want to be those who will be manifesting His Presence throughout the earth, we have to allow everything we have ever thought, hoped, believed, or felt to be placed on the altar of God. This does not necessarily mean that God will sacrifice it all. All too frequently, however, people consider God to be their spiritual smorgasbord—they can pick and choose whatever they want from God. The truth is, however, that we are His smorgasbord: we are to be laid upon the altar where He can pick and choose what He wants of us!

There are many folks who are excited about being on the cutting edge of what God is doing. Many want to be in the center of God's will and be found doing what is pleasing to Him. But few folks realize that to be on the cutting edge of what God is doing means that God has to be on the cutting edge of our hearts. We have to allow Him to cut and mold and make us into His image and into His likeness. That's what the cutting edge is all about. God's cutting edge is at work in my life. That puts me on the cutting edge of what God is doing today. Flesh must give way to spirit. Even old attitudes, hurts, and bitterness must go as the Lord Jesus purifies the habitation of our hearts for Himself.

> ...FEW FOLKS REALIZE THAT TO BE ON THE CUTTING EDGE OF WHAT GOD IS DOING MEANS THAT GOD HAS TO BE ON THE CUTTING EDGE OF OUR HEARTS.

Will we move with God? Will we respond to what God speaks? Our attitude must be like Abraham's. We have to let the Ishmael of our flesh go. "Lord, you can take whatever you want to take. You can do with me whatever you want to do. You're the one who is God!"

In our cleverness, we try to juggle both Isaac and Ishmael. That will not work. There was contention between the son of the bondwoman and the son of the free woman. When you mix flesh and spirit the result is always strife, chaos, and confusion. You'll live your life in confusion and doubt. You'll want to hang on to the old and grasp the new, but in the process everything will become discolored. In Haggai 2, we read, "You ask the priest. If you have something that's clean and you pour it into a vessel that's unclean, will you make the unclean vessel clean? And the priest said, 'No! But if you take that which is unclean and pour it into the clean, both are defiled'" (author's paraphrase).

What will make me part of what God is doing in this hour? What will make me be one of those who carry the Ark of the Presence of God on my shoulders? The bottom line is that I have to lay bare my life before Him so He can change me. There must be nothing in my life that I hold more dear than Him. Our attitude must be that He can have anything He wants— our careers, a job opportunity, whatever. The cry of our heart must be, "God, I want to be where you are more than I want to be where I am."

David said, "I thought about my life, and I decided to obey Your rules. I will hurry and not wait to obey Your commands" (Ps. 119:59-60). The Isaac and the Ishmael both exist in all our lives. When we first come to God, we come to Him as a broken person. That's why we cry out to Him; we recognize that we're broken. We see that we desperately need Him. We are transformed by the renewing of our minds (see Rom. 12:2). We become His workmanship. Likewise, the Lord is coming for a Church "that does not have stain or wrinkle or any such thing" (see Eph. 5:27). To be on the cutting edge of what God is doing in this hour, we need to give Him ourselves, that He might change us and heal us from within.

Presence Ponderings

1. God's promise is to those who are willing to cast off fleshly desires and embrace His spiritual truths.

2. Being on the cutting edge of what God is doing means that God is on the cutting edge of our hearts.

3. The Isaac in us cannot come forth until we first cast out the Ishmael.

4. To carry the Presence of God upon our shoulders, we must lay down our lives, bare, before Him.

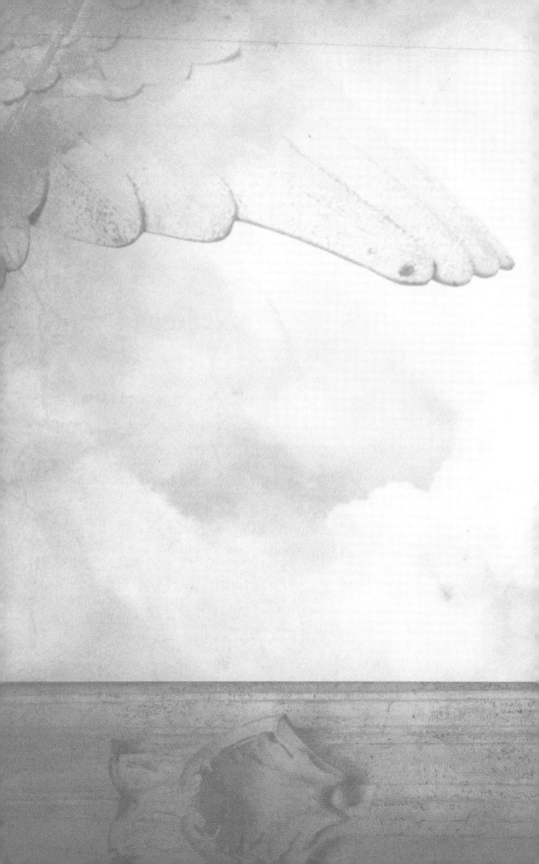

PART II

Moving to Solomon's Temple

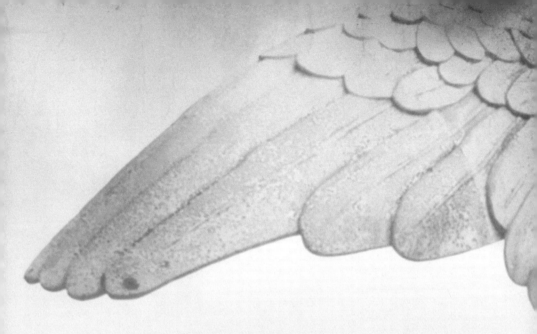

CHAPTER 6

God's Provision—Fullness
of Salvation

A House of Sacrifice

Solomon finished the temple of the Always-Present One and the royal palace. He had success in doing everything that he planned in the temple of the Always-Present One and his own palace. Then the Always-Present One appeared to Solomon at night. The Always-Present One said, "Solomon, I have heard your prayer. And, I have chosen this place for Myself to be a temple for sacrifices (2 Chronicles 7:11-12).

One of the great things lacking in the charismatic movement has been sacrifice. But anything worth receiving from God has been purchased with sacrifice, a great deal of sacrifice. In fact, the place of sacrifice is the place of fullness. The preparation for Solomon's Temple was a period of great sacrifice (see 1 Kings 5).

It would be inconsistent with the Scriptures for God to shelter those who are either wicked or lukewarm concerning Him and His purposes. God's shelter and His Manifest Presence will always be exclusively for those who have called upon Him, who love Him with undying love and whose hearts are set on fulfilling all that is on God's heart for them to do. This is the kind of people who will be able to make it in the last days. These people are not just satisfied with what they can *get* from God; the fact is they will not be satisfied until they are *doing* what is on God's heart for them to do. Good works won't suffice for them. Doing good deeds for other people won't be good enough for them. These people want to know what God's passion is for the moment and they want to fulfill that in God. They want to be a people who fulfill the heart-desire of God. What a passion! What a desire! What a fire to go through life with! God delights in these people and He says of them, "They are Mine!"

The Scriptures say,

> *The Always-Present One of the armies [of heaven] says: "They belong to Me. On that day when I take action, they will be My very own. A father spares his son who serves him. In the same way, I will spare My people. Once again, you people will see the difference between [what happens to] good people and what happens to bad people. You will see the difference between those who serve God and those who don't!"* (Malachi 3:17-18).

That fullness comes from Him. His fullness is expressed through people who are submitted to Him, who are willing to go His way and pay the price so that He may be all in all, that He may have the preeminence in all things. God wants us to experience His fullness, not in theory, but in practice.

It is too easy for us to be satisfied with what we have. We experience some things; we suffer some things and we walk into a certain depth of experience with God. We think it's satisfactory and we say, "Well, I've come far enough."

Too many of us want to proclaim: "I have fought a good fight. I have finished the race" (2 Tim. 4:7) long before we should. Many of us serve the

Lord five, ten, twenty years and think we have fought the fight, finished the course and it's all over. In reality, we have only just begun. We decide that we have suffered enough. We have paid enough of a price. We may have been a youth director for a number of years, or opened our home to a home meeting for a number of years, or ministered in one capacity or another and gone through some difficult times and some deep waters in our time of ministry. And still at a relatively young age, we may declare, "I have fought the fight, I have finished the course," and we find our "Lazy-boy" recliner, get our remote control television and end up on Sunday afternoons as a "football-aholic" without ever going on to the deep, limitless, and vast purposes of God for our lives.

> TOO MANY OF US WANT TO PROCLAIM: "I HAVE FOUGHT THE GOOD FIGHT, I HAVE FINISHED THE COURSE" LONG BEFORE WE SHOULD.

It is interesting to note how Paul weaves his preaching and his exhorting into his letter to Timothy. The Scriptures say, "For I am already being poured out as a drink offering, and the time of my departure has come. I have fought a good fight, I have finished the race, I have kept the faith" (2 Tim. 4:7). This is Paul's declaration at the end of his life, not at the end of a difficult experience early in his life. Clearly, Paul had performed and accomplished all that was on God's heart for him to do.

This Scripture is like someone who is getting on a train as it is getting ready to pull out of the station. Let's imagine that the man getting on the train is the apostle Paul. Just prior to boarding the train, the great apostle turns to speak to his young friend Timothy: "In the future, Christ will judge people who are now alive and people who have died. Because of the nearness of His appearance and His kingdom, I warn you before God and Christ Jesus: Preach the message! Be ready in good times and times that are not so good. Prove sinners wrong. Correct and comfort, with all kinds of patience and teaching" (2 Tim. 4:1-2).

He is interrupted by the whistle blowing. The train begins to chug slowly forward, and Paul jumps on the train, still calling back to Timothy: "The time will come when people will not put up with healthy teaching. Instead, following their own evil desires, they will gather themselves many, many teachers to say what they want to hear" (2 Tim. 4:3). As the train picks up speed and Timothy is running alongside, Paul shouts through the window, "And, they will turn away from listening to the truth. They will go after myths. Use self-control in everything. Endure. Do the work of the one who preaches the Good News. Finish your ministry. I am already being poured out like a drink offering. The time has come for me to die. I have fought a good fight, I have finished the race, I have kept the faith" (2 Tim. 4:4-7).

Although he declares that he has fought the fight and finished the course, his preaching and his passion and his exhortation to Timothy do not sound like the words of a man who is ready to retire. The degree of passion expressed by his words and urgency does not seem as if it is coming from a man who is finished with the ministry and is done serving the Lord.

A depth of experience yet remains for each of us in this life. When God brought the children of Israel out of Egypt, and they crossed the Red Sea, Canaan was a reality they would have been able to enjoy after only an 11-day journey. But their stubbornness, rebellion, sin, grumbling, and complaining caused them to wander for 40 years in the wilderness. Of those who left Egypt, all but two died in the wilderness, never entering into the Promised Land.

It is important to understand the fact that most people have not entered into the promise of His fullness does not negate the reality that it is there for us to attain. It is available for all who are willing to go on without grumbling and complaining, for those who are willing to fight the good fight of faith. It is these people alone who will experience the fullness of His Presence *right here in this life*. It is not more elusive, nor more futuristic than Canaan was to the children of Israel. But they made it elusive and unattainable because of their own unwillingness to submit to the miracle-working direction of the Holy Spirit in their lives.

Let us not be that kind of people. Rather, let us understand that ministering from a place of fullness, experiencing God's Presence and power in all its majesty is for us, in this life, in the here and now. It is not something we attain to in our old age, but a realm that we may enter into even at a young age. It is possible for people of all ages to flow and function in that realm all the days of their lives.

Spiritual Middle-Classism

There is a kind of cultural Christianity that once-on-fire Christians often fall into. I call this phenomenon "spiritual middle-classism." It is most often typified with words like the following: "I have come far enough. I've suffered, I've struggled, I've led my quota to the Lord in my lifetime. I'm now in my thirties, forties, or fifties, etc.; I've got two cats in the yard, three kids sitting in front of the television watching Sponge Bob, and things are pretty nice. I've got my career, everyone's healthy, I'm a Sunday school teacher, go to church at least once a week, even twice a week, and my life is pretty well settled. I'm happy; I'm content."

The fire has gone out. It is a type of Christian middle-classism, or religious Yuppie-ism. It is a satisfaction with things as they are. But there remains an incomprehensible vastness in God for those who will seek His fullness. There is a depth of relationship in fellowship with Him that only those who have a burning passion for Him will ever experience. He wants us to *run* after Him. He does not want us to be content or satisfied with what we have or what we've experienced. There is a place of shelter, a relationship, a reality of the spiritual Presence of God that is for our experience in this life that will only be attained as we yield to Him with all our heart, with all our soul, with all our mind, and with all our strength. We too easily forget there is a vastness and limitlessness that God has for us. It is His Manifest Presence and it is there for all who will respond—and keep on responding—to God's call in their lives.

> THERE IS A DEPTH OF RELATIONSHIP IN FELLOWSHIP WITH HIM THAT ONLY THOSE WHO HAVE A BURNING PASSION FOR HIM WILL EVER EXPERIENCE.

Walking in God's Fullness

Solomon was a man who, at an early age, possessed such wisdom that the kings of the earth came to see him. This extraordinary wisdom was nothing his own brain had produced, however. God poured eternal wisdom into him. Solomon had managed to tap into the eternal wisdom of God (see 1 Kings 4:29-31). There is a provision that enables us to tap into the eternal wisdom, the eternal everything of God. It is a place where people are genuinely ministered to and touched by the Lord, no matter in what state of life they may find themselves. Whether they're at home folding diapers or working outside the home, whether they're in school, no matter what they're doing—they are to be filled with all the fullness of God. When people with needs come to you, you can give them what they need from heaven. God doesn't have any other fingers but *our fingers,* He doesn't have any other voice but *our voice.* He doesn't have any ears but *our ears.* And if He is to touch the world, He will do so through people like you and me if we remain yielded to Him. He can touch the world with our hands. He can heal the sick through us. People will hear His love call through us. This is the place of fullness.

The Scriptures say that "when that which is complete comes, the parts will disappear. When I was a child, I used to talk about the things that a child would talk about. I thought and reasoned as a child does, but now that I have become an adult, I have put aside the ways of children. At this time, we see only a blurred image in the metal mirror. At the time of maturity, we will see plainly—as one person looking at another's face. Now I know things only partially, but then I will know everything completely, just as God knows me" (1 Cor. 13:10-12).

God wants us to put aside the partial so we can embrace the complete, to put aside that which is limited so we can embrace that which is unlimited. The Lord is continually saying to us, *"When will you stop being content with a gift, so that you can express Him who is all the gifts? When will you become discontent with just knowing the **partial**, when you can know Him, who is the All in All?"*

In Solomon's Temple, we see the expression of moving in the very fullness of God. "The physical body came first, not the spiritual body" (1 Cor. 15:46). In natural things, we often find examples of spiritual truths. Natural situations can frequently be spiritualized. For instance, Israel is a type of the Church. The things that happened to Israel in the Old Testament can be applied to us in the New Testament. When Israel became a nation right after World War II, it was a natural indication that spiritually we were near the close of the age, when the Lord was about to come to claim His own nation, the spiritual Israel of God.

David's Tabernacle was a place of intimacy. There was no form there; there were no rituals. Sacrifices were only made in David's Tabernacle when the Ark of the Covenant was first placed there. But after those initial sacrifices, David's Tabernacle was a place of great spontaneity. It was a place of dancing, a place where the song of the Lord could be heard. It was a place where the prophetic was as normal as breathing, where praise and worship continued day and night without the form and the ritual of the wilderness tabernacle. (See First Chronicles 16.)

Mount Gibeon, on the other hand, was a place of form. Moses' Tabernacle was there on Mount Gibeon and it was from Moses' Tabernacle that the Philistines had stolen the Ark of the Covenant. (See First Samuel 4:1-11.) So the Ark of the Covenant was not even there, for after David recovered the Ark from the Philistines, he never took it back to Mount Gibeon and Moses' Tabernacle. Instead, he brought it to David's Tabernacle on Mount Zion. So Gibeon was a place of form, the place where the priests and the Levites fulfilled the letter of the Law. It was a place where they fulfilled the daily ordinances and duties of the priesthood, but it was not a place of intimacy. It was not a place of spontaneity. And it was not a place where the Presence of God dwelt.

Only when the utensils and the form of Mount Gibeon were united with the spontaneity and life from Mount Zion and moved together into Solomon's Temple was the glory of God able to fall once again. It doesn't matter how much spontaneity and life you have. If there is no order, God's glory will not be in it. And in the same way, Mount Gibeon, with its form and its rituals and its ordinances and its many sacrifices, apart from the spontaneity and intimacy experienced at Mount Zion and David's Tabernacle cannot manifest God's life. There is no glory in such a place.

The glory of God requires responsibility so that with our spontaneity there will be purity. Intimacy and form are not mutually exclusive; there must be harmony between the two. Life without structure is no life at all. Our natural bodies are a good example of this principle. Our heartbeat, our muscles, every living cell within us thrives; blood vessels carry living blood, life-giving nourishment and oxygen to every part of our bodies. And yet, without the structure of the skeletal system, the body would be useless. By the same token, we can have a perfectly constructed skeletal system, but if there is no heart pumping blood, no veins to carry it, no muscles, no cells to contain the vibrancy of life, all you have is a good form. But there's no life.

INTIMACY AND FORM ARE NOT MUTUALLY EXCLUSIVE; THERE MUST BE HARMONY BETWEEN THE TWO.

When there is a good, solid, healthy skeletal structure and flesh and blood and a heart that beats with the vibrancy of life in one body, you have the fullness of what the human body was meant to be. And so it is in Solomon's Temple. So it is when the uniting of the spontaneity and the intimacy of David's Tabernacle and the form and the ordinances and the sacrifices of Moses' Tabernacle on Mount Gibeon combine in perfect harmony to produce the glory of God. It is so powerful and so intense that God said, "I have chosen this temple and made it holy. So, I will be worshiped here forever. Yes, I will always watch over it and love it" (2 Chron. 7:16).

Now the spiritual application is clear. God is certainly not referring to a physical place where there are physical utensils and physical sacrifices and the physical Ark of the Covenant containing the Presence of God. God was speaking in the prophetic sense, in that when you and I allow our hearts to become "Solomon's Temple" we have God's laws written in our hearts. When this happens, His laws and His ordinances become those things that we love and cherish and embrace, and our fellowship with Jesus becomes intimate and spontaneous and spectacular. There is a marriage of His character and His life within us. It is then that the fullness of God is pleased to dwell perpetually in His people.

These people are the ones who will experience the Manifest Presence of God—God's Presence manifesting itself in healing and restoration, in power and protection, and intimacy and friendship.

Intimacy and Order

In the past, there was Mount Gibeon and David's Tabernacle. There is a relationship between the two. We can see this natural/spiritual relationship as we study David's Tabernacle and Moses' Tabernacle on Mount Gibeon. When we understand these two tabernacles, we'll have a clearer picture of what God is doing for us right now in this final slice of the second millennium after Christ.

Mount Gibeon is where Moses' Tabernacle was located. In Moses' Tabernacle, there were ceremonial washings and sacrifices. There were the duties of the priesthood that cleansed the nation of Israel from their sins so that God would hear their prayers and they could have access to God. It was a daily responsibility of the priests to perform the sacrifices and the rituals and the duties of the house of the Lord in Moses' Tabernacle in order to provide the cleansing that the children of Israel needed to enter the Presence of God and experience His forgiveness. The Philistines stole the Ark of the Covenant—that beautiful golden box in which God chose to "live." Moses' Tabernacle was now empty. The Presence of God was not there (see 2 Chron. 1:3-4).

Despite this reality, the priests continued to make their sacrifices. They continued to burn their incense. They continued to go through all their forms and rituals—all the requirements of the Law, even though God's

Presence wasn't there. They were united in making certain that the system continued to go. The Presence of God was no longer in Moses' Tabernacle and neither was the Ark, but all the ceremonies and rituals that had to happen, as though God's Presence were there, continued.

Then David came along and brought the Ark of the Covenant back. But instead of bringing it back up to Mount Gibeon and putting it in Moses' Tabernacle, David brought the Ark into Jerusalem, pitched a tent in his back yard and put the Ark of the Covenant there. There was tremendous praise and worship going on in David's Tabernacle before the Ark of the Covenant while the sacrifices continued to be offered on Mount Gibeon. The legal, correct, God-given ordinances were still being followed in Mount Gibeon, but God's Presence was not there. God's Presence was in the tent that David pitched. Praise and worship were going on in David's Tabernacle.

This is the natural example: on Gibeon the God-given laws, the God-given regulations, the God-given rules were still being honored. We're not talking simply about tradition. The priests on Mount Gibeon were not doing things simply out of a sense of tradition. They were doing their God-ordained duties. They were fulfilling God-ordained rules and God-ordained regulations and offering God-ordained sacrifices. What they were doing on Mount Gibeon was of God. God had told them to do it. Although the Ark was gone, there was never a command given by God to "close down" the Tabernacle.

In David's Tabernacle, there were no curtains, no holy place, no most holyplace. It simply contained the Ark of the Covenant. The people could enter and depart freely. In David's Tabernacle there was spontaneity, there were prophetic words; there was life. There was relationship. There was intimacy, zeal, excitement, glory, and power. All the things that surround life happened in David's Tabernacle.

As we consider David's Tabernacle, we discover there was no recorded place where God told him to construct that tabernacle. The Lord gave no instructions as to how to place the Ark of the Covenant where David did or how he did. There is no record of any instructions about leaving one room the way he did.

Concerning Solomon's Temple, however, the command to build was spoken to David by the prophet Nathan. The minutest details were ordained of God. Everything had to be built according to His pattern. Everything had to be constructed according to the plan. Ultimately, that is where the glory fell (see 2 Chron. 7:1).

On Mount Gibeon, not too much that was exciting was taking place. Nonetheless, God required them to do what they were doing.

Which place do you think people of that day would flock to? To David's Tabernacle, where there was spontaneity, life, zeal, the prophetic word, God's Presence, and the excitement of being able to have intimacy with God? Or to Mount Gibeon, where there was nothing but the slaughtering of animals and the smell of burning flesh and the day-to-day work of the sacrifices? No one wanted to be on Gibeon, for sure. Everyone wanted to be at David's Tabernacle.

Some of the most exciting reading in all the Scriptures is found in First and Second Chronicles. Let's look at an important passage in First Chronicles that describes the differences between Mount Gibeon and David's Tabernacle:

> *David left Zadok the priest and the other priests who served with him in front of the Holy Tent of the Always-Present One. This was at the place of worship in Gibeon. Every morning and evening, they offered whole burnt-offerings on the altar of burnt-offerings. They did this to follow the rules written in the Teachings of the Always-Present One.*

These were the Teachings He had given Israel (1 Chronicles 16:39-40).

These verses talk about how King David continued to command the sacrifices to be offered on Mount Gibeon. Verses 37 and 38 say, concerning the Ark on Mount Zion,

> *Then David left Asaph and the other Levites there in front of the Holy Chest of the Agreement with the Always-Present One. They were to serve there every day. David also left Obed-Edom and 68 other Levites to serve with them. Hosah and Obed-Edom (the son of Jeduthun) were guards* (1 Chronicles 16:37-38).

King David continued to command the sacrifices to be offered on Mount Gibeon. The priests were commanded to continue their daily rituals and their daily responsibilities of maintaining Moses' Tabernacle. But in Mount Zion he commanded the priesthood to offer praise and worship continually. So, simultaneously, we have two things happening. The form and the God-given rituals and ordinances on Mount Gibeon were continuing, but also the spontaneity and intimacy of praise and worship were going on at Mount Zion in David's Tabernacle.

When Solomon came along, he started the construction of a house in which God's glory would be able to dwell. He started the construction of the Temple.

Finally the day arrived when the Ark was to be taken to its permanent resting place.

> *Then Solomon called for all the leaders of Israel. He asked them to come to him in Jerusalem. He called for all the elders, the heads of the tribes, and the leaders of the clans. He wanted them to bring the Holy Chest of the Covenant with the Always-Present One from the older part of the city. All the men of Israel came together with King*

Solomon. This was during the festival that was held in the 7th month. All the elders of Israel arrived. Then the Levites picked up the Holy Chest. The priests and the Levites carried the Holy Chest of the Agreement. They also carried the Holy Tent and the holy things in it (2 Chronicles 5:2-5).

All the utensils and everything they needed from Mount Gibeon were brought in and the Ark of the Covenant was brought in. And they took them together to Solomon's Temple.

King Solomon and all the Israelites met in front of the Holy Chest of the Agreement. They sacrificed so many sheep and bulls that no one could count them. Then the priests put the Holy Chest of the Covenant with the Always-Present One in its place. This was inside the Most Holy Place in the temple. They put it under the wings of the gold creatures (2 Chronicles 5:6-7).

This is an exciting and crucial passage. They carried the Ark of the Covenant only a few hundred yards from David's Tabernacle to Solomon's Temple. All that way was bathed in blood as they sacrificed sheep and oxen. So many sheep and oxen were slaughtered along that short distance that they could not be numbered.

We know that people of that day were able to count well into the hundreds of thousands, but they sacrificed so many sheep and oxen, as they traversed those few hundred yards, that they lost count. It was beyond the capacity of their numbering system. The Bible says they could not be counted. So great was their sacrifice that it was beyond their numerical system's ability to measure.

Can you imagine how much blood was shed along the way? Something of such glory, of such spontaneity, of such intimacy, all of a sudden was so blood-splattered. All of a sudden, it was coated with blood.

The route from both David's Tabernacle and Mount Gibeon to the fullness of God is a passage that is bathed with great sacrifice, beyond our ability to measure. And yet, that is what is required to experience the glory of the Lord. This truth presents us with a type of the total brokenness of man. In another aspect, we can look at it and say, David's Tabernacle is a type of intimacy, but Solomon's Temple is a type of rulership, dominion, and kingship.

From this, we learn that to move from a place of intimacy with God to a place of dominion, authority, ruling and reigning in this life takes great sacrifice. It takes the death of who I think I am. It is a way that is paved with great blood.

> ...TO MOVE FROM A PLACE OF INTIMACY WITH GOD TO A PLACE OF DOMINION, AUTHORITY, RULING AND REIGNING IN THIS LIFE TAKES GREAT SACRIFICE.

"And they drew out the staves of the ark, that the ends of the staves were seen from the ark before the oracle; but they were not seen without. And there it is unto this day" (2 Chron. 5:9 KJV). The Ark of the Covenant was carried by the priests with poles that were placed through rings on either side of it. The priests put the poles on their shoulders. When the Ark of the Covenant was made, those poles were placed in those rings and they were never removed until the Ark arrived at its permanent resting place. As soon as the Ark of the Covenant was taken to Solomon's Temple and put into its place, they pulled the staves (poles) out of the Ark, because the Ark was home. God's Presence was home, never to be moved again.

The Scriptures say that there was nothing in the Ark except the two tablets that Moses put there at Horeb, where the Lord made a covenant with the sons of Israel when they came out of Egypt. But something was missing. Aaron's rod that budded was not there. The manna was not there. (See First Kings 8:9.) What happened to those items? If we are to move into the fullness of God's purposes for you and me, there will be nothing in our hearts but God's laws written there. We serve God simply because He is God and simply because our hearts burn for Him.

Aaron's rod that budded represents our calling in life or ministry. We may be called to a ministry or called to write a book or called to raise a beautiful family, but these things in and of themselves are not what will motivate us to serve God. The manna was also missing. God's miraculous provision for us will not be what keeps us. What will keep us is our hearts burning for Him and that is by His grace. If we are to move not only into intimacy but into dominion and ruling and reigning with Jesus, we will do it because it's in our hearts to do it. We won't do it because "He called me to be a mighty leader," and we won't do it because He provides for us. We will love Him and serve Him because our heart burns after Him even if He doesn't call us to be a great leader and even if He doesn't provide the miraculous for us. I will serve Him because He's God and because I love Him and because He is worthy to be praised and glorified and served. He is the God of the universe.

And Jesus said to the multitudes, "You are looking for me, not because of the miracles but because you ate the food and were filled!" (John 6:26). But He will have a people who will follow Him whether He feeds them or not. He will have a people who follow Him just because they're passionately in love with Him. The only thing on their hearts will be His laws written there.

There cannot be any bitterness or immaturity in such people. There cannot be any greed or any power seeking. There cannot be anything that is evil. There cannot be anything in the flesh.

If we are to move in God's fullness in this life, there can be nothing in our hearts but His law. This will enable us to move from the place of intimacy in David's Tabernacle to the place of fullness and the permanent dwelling place in Solomon's Temple. First the natural and then the spiritual.

> *Then all the priests left the sanctuary. All the priests from each group made themselves ready to serve the Always-Present One. All the Levite musicians stood on the east side of the altar. They were Asaph, Heman, Jeduthun, and all their sons and relatives. They were dressed in white linen and played cymbals, lyres, and harps. With them were 120 priests who blew trumpets. Those who blew the trumpets and those who sang together sounded like one person. They praised and thanked the Always-Present One. They sang as they played their trumpets, cymbals, and other instruments. They praised the Always-Present One with this song: "The Always-Present One is good. His love continues forever!" Then the temple of the Always-Present One was filled with a cloud. The priests could not continue their work because of the cloud. This was because the Always-Present One's glory filled the temple of God* (2 Chronicles 5:11-14).

There is no record of the glory cloud appearing *in* Mount Gibeon. And in spite of all the excitement and anticipation related to David's Tabernacle, the glory cloud was never *in* David's Tabernacle. Never. The glory cloud came when the God-ordained requirements were married to the Presence of God. And with great sacrifice they were carried to Solomon's Temple. That's where the glory cloud fell.

We often hear a teaching that states or implies, "There's spontaneity here so order isn't important." I had always looked at Mount Gibeon as the old mountain, which was no good, where the priests were carnal and fleshly and so traditional they couldn't see the glory of God. They just did their rituals out of a sense of rote. In my thinking, David's Tabernacle was where "it was at."

Recently, however, I've discovered that Gibeon was not that bad a place after all! Everything they did at Gibeon was God-ordained and God-required. They were not just traditionalists. They were doing what God had commanded them to do.

What we have always called intimacy will carry us to a point, but along with intimacy, there needs to be responsibility and accountability. True intimacy can be experienced only through an abiding love relationship. An abiding love relationship produces responsibility and accountability.

Mount Gibeon was where the requirements of the Law were fulfilled. Apart from God's Presence, however, you can do what's right till you turn blue, but if you do it in your own strength, without God's Presence, there's no glory in it. You can dance and shout, praise God, prophesy, speak in tongues, and have seventy-seven banner parades, but if it's done in impurity and if it's done without the requirements of righteousness being fulfilled, there can be no glory. It takes the marriage of the righteousness of God and the requirements for God's Presence that produces a permanent, glorious dwelling place called Solomon's Temple (a place where God's glory comes forth so the earth can be filled with His glory). This gold-laden temple is within you and me.

It's not what I can shout and claim and believe for. It's what I am willing to die for. It's what you, in your heart, are broken to do that will bring forth life. Life is something that cannot be forced. Humanity cannot command life. The world craves reality and life. It craves something real to believe in. As we see the final hour quickly approaching, the world is desperate for the Lord, desperate for reality.

> IT'S NOT WHAT I CAN SHOUT AND CLAIM
> AND BELIEVE FOR. IT'S WHAT I AM WILLING
> TO DIE FOR.

As humanity's towers come down and generic glory fades, as God blinks His eye and sends wrath upon the earth, humankind will cry out for reality, even as we now see them beginning to cry out with great fervency. In the days to come, we will come to see a much greater fervency of the lost crying out to the Lord, humanity crying out for reality.

People don't want religion; they don't want philosophies; they don't want fine words; they don't want to be soothed. They want help. The world craves reality and life. There will be a people who will carry that life to them.

Only God can command life. I cannot command life in you. Either you die to yourself and let that life come forth, or no life will come forth. That's a decision that only you can make. This is the point at which it gets scary and dangerous because none of us wants to see others make the wrong choices. The bottom line is that *we* make the choices that affect our lives.

Solomon's Prayer

Solomon prayed a prayer of dedication for the Temple:

Now, O my God, I pray Thee, let Thine eyes be open, and Thine ears attentive to the prayer offered in this place. Now therefore arise, O Lord God, to Thy resting place, Thou and the ark of Thy might; let Thy priests, O Lord God, be clothed with salvation, and let Thy godly ones rejoice in what is good" (2 Chronicles 6:40-41 KJV).

Does Solomon's prayer sound like David's prophecy in Psalm 132?

The Always-Present One has chosen Jerusalem.

He wants it for His home. He says: "This is my resting-place forever. Here is where I want to stay. I will bless her. I will satisfy her poor people with food. I will let her priests receive deliverance. And, those of her who follow God will truly sing for joy! (Psalm 132:13-16).

We see the fulfillment of this prophecy in Solomon's Temple: "Now therefore, arise, O Lord God, Thou and the ark of Thy might…. O Lord God, do not turn away the face of Thine anointed; remember Thy lovingkindness to Thy servant David" (2 Chron. 6:41-42 KJV).

When the items and utensils from the tent of meeting in Mount Gibeon and the Presence of God from David's Tabernacle made their way to Solomon's Temple, and the Ark of the Covenant was brought into the most holy place, a sacrifice was laid on the altar. Solomon had prayed his prayer of dedication. As they were giving him the fire and he was ready to light the fire that would burn the sacrifice he had prepared for God, something else happened. Somebody else lit that fire.

When Solomon finished praying, fire came down from the sky. It burned up the whole burnt-offering and the sacrifices. The Always-Present One's glory filled the temple. The priests could not enter the temple of the Always-Present One, because the Always-Present One's splendor filled it. All the people of Israel saw the fire come down from heaven. They also saw the Always-Present One's glory on the temple. Then they bowed down on the pavement with their faces to the ground. They worshiped and thanked the Always-Present One. They said, "The Always-Present One is good! His love continues forever!" (2 Chronicles 7:1-3)

Obedience Is the Key

There is a way to move into God's fullness. There *is* a way to experience His Presence and His power. That is simply to walk in obedience. You have to respond in obedience to the Lord and move in the light of His Presence and allow God to establish Himself in you.

Putting our flesh in subjection to the Spirit of God and allowing Jesus to be Lord is the only way His ultimate purpose will be fulfilled in us. When our hearts are submitted to Him, then He receives our song, our worship, our dance, our talents, and our abilities. Wonderful communion follows!

This is moving from a place of intimacy to a place of intimacy *and* responsibility. It is accomplished through grave sacrifice, a sacrifice so great that it can't be measured. That's where the cloud of glory will fall, if we do not resist what God wants to do. We have to allow the sacrifice to be made. And that is where we will begin to experience the day-by-day fullness of the lifestyle that is called being "born again."

We move from the place of just hanging on to go to Heaven, to a place where God's Presence, His power, and His fullness flow through us like a river, watering the whole earth. It is the place of His Manifest Presence.

> WE MOVE FROM THE PLACE OF JUST HANGING ON TO GO TO HEAVEN, TO A PLACE WHERE GOD'S PRESENCE, HIS POWER, AND HIS FULLNESS FLOW THROUGH US LIKE A RIVER, WATERING THE WHOLE EARTH.

There is a valid church system where people are performing the work of the ministry—they're teaching the Word; they're fulfilling the requirements of order and respect—but there's no presence of God. They're doing what needs to be done; they're keeping the mechanics of the church going, but there's no glory because God isn't there. Let's compare those good folks to the priests of Mount Gibeon.

On the other hand, there are those churches who experience the Manifest Presence of God all the time, which for these purposes, I am tying together with David's Tabernacle. These good folks move in great spontaneity, with great glory, great intimacy, the fruit of the Spirit, and everything connected with it. They even have an element of order, but the system in itself doesn't bring God's glory.

What we've experienced thus far in the charismatic movement has not really brought God's glory down to establish a place of permanence. The Church is now at the point where God is bringing together what we have traditionally known as the charismatic movement and that which He ordained out of the "traditional" church so that we can walk into God's fullness.

"...during the last days...people will hold the outer form of religion, but they say no to its inner power" (2 Tim. 3:1-5). These people will know all the right things to say and do, but there will be no power to bring it to pass. Godliness becomes form when the life of God is absent.

On the other side, under the banner of the charismatic movement, we see the truth that John revealed, "He was the Source of life. That life was light for people. The light shines in the darkness; the darkness can never put it out!" (John 1:4-5).

Joel said,

God says: "In the last days, I will pour out My Spirit upon all people. Your sons and your daughters will prophesy. Your young men will see visions. Your old men will have special dreams. At that time, I will pour out My Spirit upon My servants, both men and women, and they will prophesy (Acts 2:17-18).

Spontaneity and life need to be married to godliness. Godliness becomes a lifestyle of vibrant holiness when genuine order is introduced to a genuinely spiritual experience.

David's Tabernacle and Mount Gibeon come together in Solomon's Temple. There, life is restored to the form that God ordained, so that we can get a true picture of who God is: an intimate, loving, gentle, compassionate, lovely God who is just and holy and righteous and pure. He wants all things to be done decently and in order.

We need to marry the life and vibrancy of our experience of the Holy Spirit to the discipline, holiness, and doctrines of the Scriptures to experience the true fullness of God.

In the Book of Hebrews, we read that "Jesus endured when He had to suffer shame and die on a cross…" (Heb. 12:2). The issue is not whether to preach David's Tabernacle or Solomon's Temple, but Jesus says, "I am the way, and the truth, and the life" (John 14:6). When Jesus said, "I am the way," He referred to the way being God's plan. When He said, "I am the truth," He referred to the truth being the law of Gibeon. When He said, "I am the life," He referred to Himself.

When these powerful elements come together—the way, the truth, and the life—the fullness of the Godhead is there. God's plan, His way, is to have the truth and the life coming together, so that we can have a true picture of who He is. This will also give us a true picture of what God really has for us. This will bring His Manifest Presence into our midst.

When everyone placed so much emphasis on God's character to the exclusion of other truths, we were brought back to Mount Gibeon. We preached, "This is how you're supposed to act, this is how a family is sup-posed to be, this is the way it's supposed to be done." Too often, however, our preaching was done without an emphasis on the life of God. Our burden is that God's character should be married to His power so that we can have a full picture of who God is and what God wants to do in our lives.

Since faith comes by hearing, we need to hear before we can become. A full picture of God's plan for us will unfold as God shows the need for inti-macy and holiness in rulership. This is where His Presence is pleased to flourish and where His love is manifest for all the world to see.

The Way to Fullness

This, then, is what God wants to do in you: He wants to bring you to a place of fullness. He wants to bring you to "Solomon's Temple," a place of fullness within your heart. But remember, that place of fullness is bathed in blood. The place where God's character is married to His power and is birthed in your mortal bodies is bathed in *your* blood. The sacrifice of Cal-vary has been made, and the door has been opened for you. But you also must die, so that His character and His power can be married in you, so that His glory can come forth and His Presence be manifested.

> THE PLACE WHERE GOD'S CHARACTER IS MARRIED TO HIS POWER AND IS BIRTHED IN YOUR MORTAL BODIES IS BATHED IN *YOUR* BLOOD.

You are the one who must decide if you will change. No one can make that decision for you. The Scriptures tell us that Jesus gave His life willingly (see John 10:17-18). Nobody *took* His life. He *gave* it willingly. Nobody made Him die on the Cross. He did it because He wanted to.

It's the same with you and me. We can be encouraged, we can be exhorted, but individually we must willingly lay ourselves on the altar of sacrifice. That's not something you simply do physically; it's something you do mentally and emotionally so that you're not just going through the motions.

Did Jesus think, "I can't believe I'm doing this! I can't believe I'm going to the Cross! I must be making a mistake! I can't understand why I have to do this"? Do you think such an attitude crossed His mind even once?

In examining ourselves, however, do attitudes like these ever cross our minds? It's not what we *do* so much: all too frequently it's what we *think* that holds us back. When He has our minds, He has *us*. When we surrender our resistance to His working, His character can truly be married to His power and it can be birthed in us and we can freely move from either camp— Mount Gibeon or David's Tabernacle.

He has chosen *us* for His abiding place! The Book of Hebrews tells us that Jesus appeared the first time bearing sin, but He will appear the second time unto salvation (see Heb. 9:26-28). *And what we see in the natural here, in absolute, literal reality, happens in the spirit.* There is no longer a Solomon's Temple, but there *is* a sanctuary of God where you and I can live and minister from the very Presence of God.

Where, then, do we begin? And how do I begin to see the coming together of David's Tabernacle and Moses' Tabernacle into Solomon's Temple in my own life?

Sometimes, we think that the spontaneity of praise and worship takes care of a lot of other things we should be doing. For instance, if we don't have time to really sit down and pray and really seek the Lord, we'll pray on the run, or at the next meeting, we'll shout a little louder and pray a little louder.

Yet, we must understand that to develop a deep and abiding walk with God, simply waving our hands, dancing at the meetings, and singing worship songs to the Lord is not enough. We need to be personally spending time with the Lord in the quiet of our own hearts. That is the way we begin to combine David's Tabernacle and Moses' Tabernacle.

It is likewise essential for us to realize that God's Presence dwells in purity. The charismatic movement has had a lot of praise and worship but not a lot of teaching about purity. God wants us to be pure. He wants us to be holy. He wants us to walk with Him in purity of motive, purity of heart.

Our mental attitudes form another area of responsibility. How we think is important. On the one hand, we're people who want to witness and share and talk about God's love, but we also need to bridle our tongues so that we're not gossips and busybodies. As God is allowed to use our tongues to share the Gospel with others, we must not permit the enemy to use our tongues to tear down and to divide and to destroy.

We often like to have our spirits soar in worship and praise, but our spirits need to be under control when our children do things that anger us. Our faith must be visible, not just in tongues and prophecy in a meeting, but it must be visible in our homes before our children, where no one else sees us. If I act differently in church than I do at home, then I'm probably a lot closer to David's Tabernacle than I am to Mount Gibeon. Our praise and worship may be spectacular and spontaneous, but if I allow Mount Gibeon to have its influence, I begin to understand the responsibility that requires me to live the kind of life that I sing and shout about in church.

This leads us to the next step in our consideration of making the Lord's Presence manifest in our lives. How do we carry His Manifest Presence? The lives of Abraham, Isaac, and Jacob have much to show us about this.

Presence Ponderings

1. Far too many want to proclaim, "I have fought the good fight," long before the battle has even begun.

2. The promise is available to all who are willing to go forth and attain it while leaving grumbling and complaining behind.

3. Just as the route from David's Tabernacle and Mount Gibeon to God's fullness was bathed in sacrifice, so must we make spiritual sacrifices today in order to experience the full manifestation of God's glory.

4. As humanity's façade of glory tumbles to the ground, the cloud of God's glory will begin to move over the earth.

5. The way to move in God's Presence and power is simply to walk in obedience.

6. We can be encouraged and exhorted, but ultimately, we are the only ones who can make the decision to change—by having a willingness to lay ourselves on the altar of sacrifice.

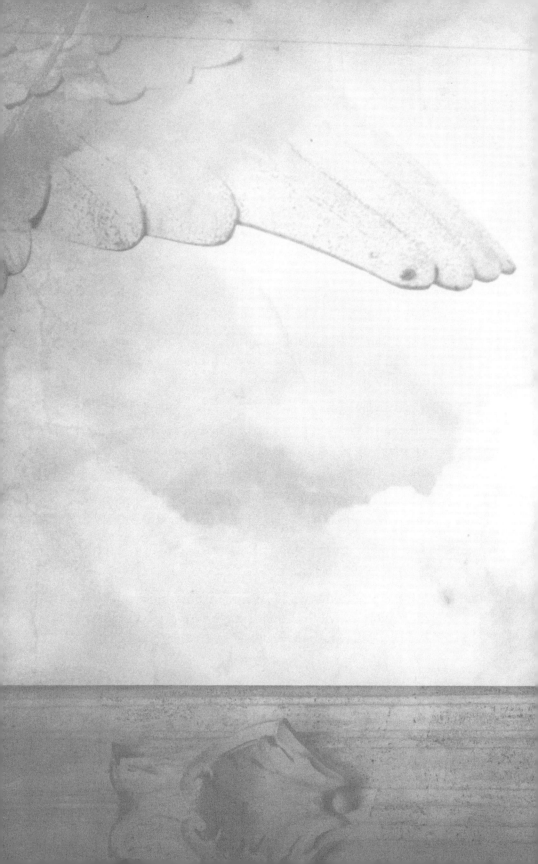

PART III

Fit for the Master's Use

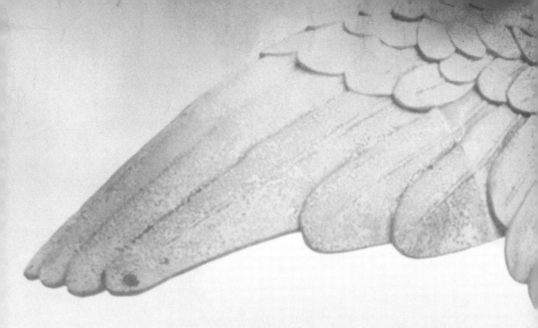

CHAPTER 7

God's Workmanship—
Changing the Inner Realm

Fulfilling Our Heart's Desire

The eternal hallmark of a people who are walking with God is their openness to change through a vital, viable, real heart relationship with God. These aren't just superficial church members who walk into a meeting and praise the Lord and walk out of the meeting and curse their neighbors. Rather, they are interested in far more important matters—they are after the purposes of God's heart. It's not how they talk, it's not even how they act, but it's the fact that they are looking for all God has for them and can do through them that counts.

This is where the real issue of intimacy comes in. God has always wanted a people with whom He could fellowship, a people with whom He could be friends.

He has always looked for a people with whom, like Adam, He could walk in the cool of the day. God's heart is after our hearts, that we may have personal fellowship and friendship with Him. Everything else we can ever accomplish, every gift, every ministry, every call we can have from God is dwarfed by comparison with this most-high calling: to walk and fellowship and be friends with the Creator of the universe.

God is looking for a people who are giving themselves to Him for change in their innermost beings. The innermost being is where God dwells. His sanctuary is our heart, where His laws are written, where His Presence begins to be manifested in our lives. Without that, we've lost it. Without that, all our meetings are meaningless. Only an encounter with the living God will produce change. The disciples of John came to Jesus while John was in prison and asked, "Are you the One who is coming, or should we expect someone else?" (see Matt. 11:2). Did Jesus say, "You go back and tell John what you see. We just added a new educational wing to the synagogue. You go back and tell John what you saw. We have the most popular church in Jerusalem"? Of course not. Jesus replied, "Go tell John the things you see and hear. The blind people can see again. Crippled people can walk. People with leprosy are made well. The deaf can hear. Dead people are given life. And the Good News is given to the poor people" (Matt. 11:4-5). When John received that report, his heart must have greatly rejoiced. In effect, Jesus was saying to him, "The Kingdom of God has come near." Matthew 11 simply repeats Isaiah 35 and Isaiah 62. Jesus said, "You go tell John that the Scriptures have been fulfilled."

> HIS SANCTUARY IS OUR HEART, WHERE HIS LAWS ARE WRITTEN, WHERE HIS PRESENCE BEGINS TO BE MANIFESTED IN OUR LIVES.

God *is* at work among people. God *is* changing people. God is coming near to earth, and His Kingdom *is* being established. There *are* people who are speaking His prophetic truth. Jesus wanted John to know,

"I am speaking and things are happening. Change is occurring. There's evidence, not just through my persuasive speech, but there is evidence from Heaven that I am who I say I am."

We are living in an age that is so skeptical and doubting that if there is to be an ingathering of people and an outpouring of the Holy Spirit such as has been prophesied, it will be because God Himself will demonstrate His own power and life from Heaven, and not because we have a great program. It will not be because we have such elegant surroundings. If there is to be a vital Holy Ghost restoration of His people, it will be because God Himself will come down and demonstrate His power in the earth. It will be because men and women yield to God from their innermost beings.

Our prayer must be, "Lord Jesus, let that come to pass. Lord Jesus, stay on the cutting edge of my heart. Change me so that I might be one of those who will see Your coming. Let me be one of those who is willing to take up Your Presence. When you say it's time to break camp, when You say, 'I'm moving,' I want to be ready to move."

We must be willing to lay aside our preconceived doctrines and traditions, yes, the most deadly of traditions—even the charismatic ones! Have you ever moved and found that you've taken everything you've accumulated through the years with you? Of course not! As you sorted through your belongings you may have given something away or even had a yard sale. However you disposed of the excess baggage, it had to happen. Otherwise, moving day would have been much longer and harder than necessary.

It's time we had some spiritual yard sales! It's time to move. Let's clean out the attic. Clean out the basement and find out what we don't need to take with us.

IT'S TIME WE HAD SOME SPIRITUAL YARD SALES!

Let's discard all that is man's ritual and tradition. Let's lay aside the false and embrace the real. Let's repent of facades and hypocrisy, approaching God in purity and sincerity. We must let God speak to our hearts and show us what must go.

Vessels Without Cracks

The Latin word from which we get the word *sincere* literally means, "without wax."[1] If you walked up to somebody and said, "I am sincere," you would actually be saying, "I am without wax." It doesn't mean you cleaned your ears out this morning. It goes a lot deeper than that. Let me explain.

In earlier times when potters made their pottery, they would either put it in the oven or set it out in the sun to dry. Oftentimes, the pottery would crack. If the potter was good, and he noticed a crack in the vessel, he would throw it away and make another one. But if the potter was unscrupulous, and he noticed a crack in the vessel, he would fill up the crack with wax. At first glance, you wouldn't have been able to tell that there was anything wrong with it. You might have bought it and tried to use it, but before long the wax would come off and you'd realize it wasn't a good piece of pottery after all. To counteract such shoddy business practices, shops began to put up signs that read, "Without wax—sincere." In other words, they began to guarantee their pottery.

God is looking for a people who are "without wax" so that He can put us in the fire, even in the furnace of affliction if need be. When we go through the trial and come out on the other side, a puddle of wax will not remain as we walk away from the fire. There will be no cracks in our vessel. We will be clean and pure, We will be fit for the Master's use, ready for every good work.

If we don't let the Ishmael (the flesh) go from our lives as God tries to deal with us, it will hold us back from what He wants for us. The Ishmael will distort our vision and cause us to walk in confusion. In such a state, we'll never really come into the things God wants for us.

God, in His mercy, begins to put us through the fires of affliction. He does this because He doesn't want us to go through life with cracks in our vessels. He doesn't want me to be "cracked" for the rest of my life. He wants to heal me. He wants to put me back together. He wants me to be genuine and real, so that His Presence can be purely manifested in me.

God puts us through the fire to cause that which is insincere to come to the surface. When those things come to the surface, our response should be, "Lord Jesus, I repent. Deal with me. Lord Jesus, heal that hurt within me. Lord Jesus, change me so I can be restored." Cracked vessels can't carry the Presence of God. Ask the Lord to deal with the hypocrisy within.

I hear so many people say about a problem in their lives, "This is my Cross. This is my weakness. This is the area in which I will fail the rest of my life." That simply does not have to be true. No matter what is broken inside of us, God can touch it and heal it, and it's His desire to do that. If we are His, we want to carry on what God is doing. We want to be vessels fit for the Master's use. We want to be a priesthood that carries the Ark of God. "Lord Jesus, put us in the fires of affliction, and show us where the wax is. Show us where the hypocrisy is. Show us where the cracks are, that we can be restored, that we can be changed."

If we don't understand what God is doing in us, we might be fearful. When God shows us something, and we see an area of weakness in our lives, He has us in the fire. Our first tendency may be to go off into the corner and rewax our vessel.

Someone may ask at such a time, "How are you doing?"

We may answer, "Praise the Lord, just fine," and we say to ourselves, *Got my vessel rewaxed; I'm under control. Hallelujah!*

Then, a while later, something else happens, the wax melts away and you have to go off into the corner again and apply more wax before you can come back out. God says, "*You don't have to do that. Come to me and I will change you. I will repair the crack forever.*" There can be restoration and healing for us from within so that we can be those who carry His Manifest Presence. The weaknesses and the sins that so easily beset us, that keep us down to drive us into the dirt, can be dealt with, and we can be healed and restored so that we don't have to carry those anymore.

If you let someone close enough to you, they will see you whenever you crack. They will see you when the wax melts away. If they love you, they're not too likely to let you wax it back up. Let it be healed. I once knew a man who said, "God just called me to be a floater. I travel around the country, spend two years here, two years there, and as soon as somebody gets too close, it's God telling me to pack my bags and go."

I said, "Hmm...I'm glad God didn't call me to be a floater."

What the floater was saying is, "Every time someone begins to see a flaw in my vessel, it's time to leave, lest anybody see more of it or it ever be dealt with." Such a man will never know the freedom that comes from allowing God to change him.

God is constructing in us a spiritual habitation for His Presence so that He can send us anywhere in the world and let any storm or any trial come upon us. In spite of the circumstances, His Presence continues to flow out of us. When this happens, we are ministering from the sanctuary of the Lord, from His fullness. He's causing us to be equipped vessels who are fit for the Master's use so that He can put us into service. There are trials and storms involved in building His Kingdom. The vessel sent to the mission field or the vessel sent to be a pastor which has cracks in it will not be very effective in building God's Kingdom. That's why God works on us and says, "Let Me heal those flaws. Let Me restore those cracks so that you can be a vessel that is fit for the Master's use."

There's a provision for our total redemption so that the things that have affected us in the past don't need to continue to affect us for the rest of our lives. Some, for example, were abused when they were children, but the hurt and pain from that mistreatment does not have to continue throughout their lives. Jesus suffered on the Cross so that we might find a place of healing. We can be effective in many areas of ministry. However, the area where we have been hurt or where we were abused, where we fell into sin or were intensely weak, may continue to be an area of weakness for us. Again, in Christ we must allow the healing power of the Holy Spirit to go deep inside. There, true repentance must be made so that the healing power of God can flow through us.

Remember this Scripture?

At that time, people will no longer say: "The fathers have eaten sour grapes. And that caused the children to grind their teeth from the sour taste." But each person will die for his own sin. The person who eats sour grapes will grind his own teeth (Jeremiah 31:29-30).

This is a covenant promise! God does not intend you to suffer for the sins of your parents, nor does He intend you to become an alcoholic because your parents were. The fact that your parents were abusive does not mean you will be an abusive parent. An unyielding, critical heart in your background, in a teacher, or a relative, should not cause you to be that way, because in Christ there is healing and repentance. The sin is ours when we fail to go God's way. We cannot blame our own sins on our past or on our parents. We must bear that responsibility. When we do, the Bible promises us forgiveness and healing so that we can walk on in wholeness, with no cracks in the vessel that will hinder us in the work of the Lord.

If we allow the Lord to do this within us, we won't leak when the pressure comes. We will be able to retain His anointing and retain His Presence and His power. Walking on in confidence and victory, we will be able to stand before God and before men with a pure heart, pure motives, and a pure spirit.

Not long ago a man came to me for counseling. As I talked with him I could tell that something was really tearing him apart. It was gnawing away at him, consuming his very life. I started asking him about his family and where he grew up and other matters pertaining to his background. He told me, "I had five brothers and sisters and a five-year-old brother who died."

"How did your brother die?" I inquired.

The man slowly began to relate a tragic story of how, when he was 12 years old, his mother asked him to go to the grocery store, two blocks away from their home. (They lived in a metropolitan area.) He decided to take his 5-year-old brother with him.

As they were walking to the store, he was distracted by a friend with whom he began to carry on a conversation. Right in front of him, his small brother darted across the street. A car sped down the street at the same time and this young man stood by helplessly as he watched his 5-year-old brother being struck by the car. The injuries were fatal.

The man wept as he related the pain he had carried during the previous 20 years. He carried such a heavy burden of guilt. He was a Spirit-filled, born-again Christian in great pain; he was hurting and wrestling with guilt. He explained, "In the last twenty years since my little brother died, there hasn't been one smile in my home. There hasn't been one day of peace in my home. Just nothing but guilt and torment and anger and strife." This big, husky, strong man broke down and sobbed.

"My people are crushed. So I am crushed. I cry loudly, and I am afraid for them" (Jer. 8:21). Yes, God's people are broken and hurting. We come out of the world, we come out of the realm of darkness, and we are knocked, bumped, scraped, bruised, and broken by the things of this world. God doesn't expect us to come to Him in perfection. That's why the Scriptures say that Jesus was bruised for our iniquities; He was chastised for our peace (see Isa. 53:5).

When I began to minister to this man, he drew back. He took a deep breath and pushed the pain down again, and he has never let me bring it up again. If only he had responded to the ministry the Lord had for him to receive! The Scriptures say,

> *Then the blind people will see again. Then the deaf will hear. Crippled people will jump like deer. And, those who cannot talk now will shout with joy. Springs of water will gush forth in the desert. Streams will flow in the dry land. The burning desert will have pools of water. The dry ground will have springs. Where wild dogs once lived, grass and water plants will grow* (Isaiah 35:5-7).

Did you ever feel like a scorched dry land? I know the hurt. I know the things I've suffered and the things God confronts me with that I have to deal with. I can remember very painful experiences in high school. If I was burned once, I was burned five hundred times by the different groups in school who would talk to me one day and laugh at me the next. I know the pain of having some guys talk to me and then, as soon as their friends came by, turn around and ignore me. In front of their friends, they didn't want to be associated with me and didn't want to talk like they knew me.

I couldn't wait to get out of school because of this phoniness. To this day, the area in which the Lord deals with me most involves trusting other men. It's hard for me to believe that people aren't just out to get me. In some ways, my expectation has been that people will be with me today, and tomorrow they'll stab me in the back! In spite of this weakness, however, I realize that if I am to be on the cutting edge of what God is doing today, I have to let Him deal with me about this, even if that means that what I fear most will happen to me! There's no way I can minister effectively if I always worry that someone will come out and turn against me.

If we are to walk the way God wants us to walk, these things from our pasts have to come out. They have to be healed. We need to be restored. We need to have the blood of Jesus cleanse us in each of these areas. It's easy to say, "God's leading me somewhere else." But before long you will discover that the problems surface wherever you go. Like the brother who felt he was called to "float," you don't allow God to change you from within.

> IF WE ARE TO WALK THE WAY GOD WANTS US TO WALK, THESE THINGS FROM OUR PASTS HAVE TO COME OUT. THEY HAVE TO BE HEALED.

Jeremiah looked out and saw God's people, and I think God gave him a heart of His own compassion. He said, "My people are crushed. So, I am crushed. I cry loudly, and I am afraid for them" (Jer. 8:21). Then he says, "Surely there is a balm in the land of Gilead. Surely there is a doctor there!? So, why aren't the hurts of my people healed? (Jer. 8:22). Jeremiah saw the condition, looked up to God and asked, "Is there no physician? Is there no healing for this?"

God replied, "Yes, there is. Yes, there is restoration. Yes, vessels can be restored and rendered without wax."

If we are to walk with God, we must change. God wants us to be conformed to His image and likeness so that we can carry His anointing, His Presence, and His power wherever we go. We need to stay close to one another, close to a pastor, close to the Word, and close to our spouse and children. We need to allow God to deal with us, without our running from Him.

We move with God by coming to Him with open hands, not holding any attitudes or doctrines or traditions that would hinder us. We must be willing to surrender our most valued opinions. Our prayer must be, "Lord, anything you want to change in me, change. Make me pliable. Make me into a new wineskin, a fresh wineskin. Change me into one who is pliable, open to change."

Then, as we come to Him and He shows us things He wants to change, as He tries to deal with the hurt that is within us, we let Him do it. We let Him heal us. We let Him change us. We let Him love us that way. When this happens, and God is ready to move, we can say, "Hallelujah," and just pack up our bags and go with Him. We are strangers and sojourners in the land. Nothing of this world is ours. We can lay claim to nothing in this life.

Our attitude must be, "There is nothing in this world that entices me, that holds me down. There's nothing that draws my attention away from you, Lord, not even a mountain that I don't think I can overcome. I am willing and able to move and to change and allow you to change me within." Jesus will honor that prayer. He will fill you with His Manifest Presence even as He filled Solomon's Temple with His glory.

ENDNOTE

1. Sincere, (2008) Merriam-Webster Online Dictionary, Retrieved December 13, 2008, from http.www.merriam-webster.com/dictionary/sincere.

Presence Ponderings

1. We are living in an age of skepticism where God, Himself, will pour out His Spirit and demonstrate His power.

2. God is looking for a sincere people; those without wax who He can put in the fire and withstand the tests and fiery trials of time.

3. God allows us to go through the trials of affliction because He doesn't want us cracked for the rest of our lives.

4. If we plan to walk in the will of God, we must allow our past to come out and healing to enter and restore those things which have been broken.

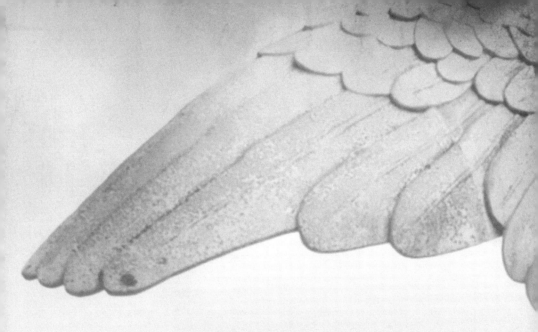

CHAPTER 8

God's Goal—The Restoration of Hearts

Freedom of Expression

There has been a tendency to make apologies for the way things go in a particular meeting, thinking that perhaps one or two people who don't understand what's going on, could be upset by certain things that take place.

There is a tendency to restrict or control the free flow of worshipful expression before the Lord. Labeling such freedom as emotionalism or extremism, such folks deprive the Lord of the genuine and intimate love flow He wants. It also deprives the people of their need to express a love that gloriously overflows from within.

Since I became a father, however, I've developed a new understanding about this concern. I have five little boys, ages eleven, nine, seven, five, and two months. One of the most exciting times for me each day is when I come home from work. My four older sons come running through the screen door and out to the car with their hands waving. "Daddy's home! Daddy's home!" they shout. They proceed to jump on me, lavishing their hugs and kisses on me. Naturally, I just love it.

How much more must our heavenly Father take delight in our joyous response to His Presence? How it must bless Him to see us standing before Him and rejoicing. The Scriptures tell us we can even call Him "Abba"—Daddy (see Rom. 8:15).

Now, those of us who are under a new covenant and have been washed in the blood of the Lamb certainly ought to be able to enter into the Presence of the Lord with joy and excitement and with expectation! The Lord loves for us to show Him how much we love Him. He wants us to enter His Presence with thanksgiving and His courts with praise.

The old, stiff orthodoxy tells us to be very somber in worship. What would I think if I'd come home from work and my little boys would stand there by the door ready to shake my hand, saying, "Good evening, Father. It's so nice to have you home tonight." It would be terrible.

In the same vein, it would be terrible for me to come home from work, have my children joyously greet me, "Daddy's home! Daddy's home! Daddy's home!" and for me to respond, "Don't be so emotional! How dare you be emotional?" To say the least, that would dampen their enthusiasm and joy!

There's nothing wrong with being emotional with somebody you love. It would be a very dull marriage if I were never emotional with my wife—very dull indeed.

We must continue to shake off the stiffness of orthodoxy and enter into God's Presence with joy and excitement, knowing that He loves us and comes alive when we run to Him, just like I get excited when my kids run to me.

> WE MUST CONTINUE TO SHAKE OFF THE STIFFNESS OF ORTHODOXY AND ENTER INTO GOD'S PRESENCE WITH JOY AND EXCITEMENT...

We Need to Know Where We Are Going

The Scriptures tell us: "Where there is no vision, the people perish" (Prov. 29:18 KJV). If you're going on vacation, you don't just pack the car, hop in, and take off. You have a destination in mind. You know *where you're going*. In this hour, the Church needs to know *where it's going*. It needs to know what is being built. The Church needs to know the determination that's in the heart of God to perform what He desires.

Let's take a closer look at that divine determination as it is depicted in Deuteronomy. Let's remember that the Old Testament is contained in the New, and the New Testament is contained in the Old. There are very vital and beautiful principles in the Old Testament.

In Deuteronomy 6, we see some of the New Testament reflected. Beginning with verse 20, we see Moses speaking to the people and instructing them regarding how they should respond to their children when they ask their parents about the exodus from Egypt and related matters. We read,

> *In the future, your son will ask you: "What is the meaning of the testimonies, the laws, and the rules which the Always-Pres-*

ent One, our God, has commanded us?" Then you will tell your son: "We were slaves to Pharaoh in Egypt. But the Always-Present One brought us out of Egypt by His great power. The Always-Present One performed great and awesome signs and miracles. He did them to Egypt, to Pharaoh, and to his whole family—right in front of our very eyes! Yes, the Always-Present One brought us out of there. He wanted to bring us here to give us the land which He vowed to our ancestors" (Deuteronomy 6:20-23).*

There is a promise in this passage that we need to embrace. Jesus did not save you to leave you in the wilderness. Jesus didn't die on the Cross and suffer so much to change you only halfway. Jesus didn't save you to leave you desolate. He didn't save you to leave you confused. He didn't save you to leave you unhealed, to leave you broken in mind, broken in spirit, and broken in heart.

The Determination of God's Heart

There is determination in the heart of God. He did not bring us out of the kingdom of darkness to leave us in spiritual limbo. He brought us out of the kingdom of darkness in order to place us into the Kingdom of His beloved Son. Every Christian needs to know that it is God's desire, purpose, and intention for His last-day people not to live in the wilderness but to come out of Egypt and to allow Jesus, through His Holy Spirit, to plant us firmly and root us in His Kingdom. It is there that we will experience His Manifest Presence.

In God's heart, there is the kind of determination that won't permit Him to start something He never intends to finish. When God determines that something will happen, *it happens*. He brought us out to take us in. He brought us out of the kingdom of darkness to translate us into the Kingdom of Light. God kept exhorting Moses and dealing with the children of Israel time after time by telling them not to grow weary, not to grow lax, not to give up, not to lose heart, not to grumble in unbelief. In effect, He admonished them, "Don't grumble, don't complain, don't give up, don't compromise. Don't be satisfied with anything less than the promised land."

God speaks to us the same way today. He says, *"Don't be complacent. Don't give up."* He gives us this encouragement because it is His intention to translate us from the kingdom of darkness into the Kingdom of the beloved Son of God, where intimacy begins and rulership is the goal—ruling and reigning with Him, allowing Jesus the Lord to manifest Himself in our flesh in this life.

Also in Deuteronomy we catch a glimpse of the heart cry of God: "Why? Because you are a holy people to the Always-Present One, your God. The Always-Present One, your God, has chosen *you* out of all the ethnic groups on the surface of the earth to be His very own" (Deut. 7:6). Another rendering of this passage reads as follows: "for you are a holy people to the Lord your God; the Lord your God has chosen you to be His own special treasure out of all the peoples on the face of the Earth."

It is tremendously exciting to know that God's purposes never change. His people are still His own special treasure. One of the driving burdens of my heart is to fulfill all that is on the heart of the Lord Jesus for my life. Can you think of anything that could be more pleasing to the Lord than to want with all your heart to fulfill everything that He has planned for you? To be everything He wants you to be?

Every one of us would have to be in a pretty radical state of rebellion to say that we don't want to be everything God wants us to be. The good news is that we *can* be everything He wants us to be and that it's His desire to bring it to pass in us. The Scriptures say, "Don't be afraid, little flock, your heavenly Father wants to give you the kingdom" (Luke 12:32). It is also the Father's good pleasure to plant you into the Kingdom of His beloved Son. It's not a mystical thing that I will spend a lifetime trying to pull out of the air. His purpose for me is a practical, day-to-day purpose that's real and tangible. It is God's intention and His pleasure to lead me into it. It's God's intention and pleasure to lead you into that same thing.

The story of the Triumphal Entry of Jesus into Jerusalem (see John 12:12) tells us so much. The Pharisees were getting a little excited because there were so many people praising the Lord. They went to Jesus and said, "Hey, can you tell these guys to cool it a little bit? Just tell them to quiet down." Jesus looked at them and replied, "If these be silent, the stones themselves will cry out." See the determination? God *will* have a people in this hour. He *will* have a people who will do all that is in His heart for them to do. He *will* have a people who exist to worship Him and praise Him. It's our choice whether we want to be a part of that people. They will dwell in His Presence.

GOD *WILL* HAVE A PEOPLE IN THIS HOUR.

The Heart of Restoration Is the Restoration of Hearts

When Moses received the Ten Commandments, it was no accident that God etched them on stone. Why didn't He use a wax tablet? Why didn't He use a clay tablet? Why did He choose stone? It could be because God equates the heart of man with stone. The unregenerate heart is made of stone.

John the Baptist said in Matthew 3:9, "Don't think you are the children of Abraham just because you are of his lineage. I tell you, God is able to raise up from these stones children of Abraham" (author's paraphrase).

It is possible that Jesus was looking at the Gentiles instead of actual stones. Unregenerate hearts are stony hearts. The Scriptures tell us that God etched the Ten Commandments on the stone tablets (see Exod. 24:12). The Scriptures also declare that His desire is to etch His laws on hearts of flesh (see Jer. 31:33). You see, He wants us to serve Him out of desire, not out of compulsion. His true people will serve the Lord because they want to, not because they're fearful of the flames of hell and not because they're being forced to obey any laws or ordinances. His people will obey willingly, even lay down their lives willingly as Jesus did (see John 10:17-18).

The Spirit of the Lord has entered into them and has so melted their hearts and their spirits that their stony hearts are turned into hearts of flesh. Just as God etched the commandments on the tablets of stone, now He would come into the hearts of men and women and etch His law on the tablets of their hearts. It is this that enables people to serve Him out of desire and not out of compulsion.

The Kingdom of God comes not with observation. It doesn't matter how fine or how mighty, holy, and righteous we look on the outside. God looks upon the heart. He wants to create a people who look alike on the inside regardless of how they look on the outside. The whole crux of the restoration movement, where we see the heart of God restoring structure and ministries and worship, is the restoration of hearts. *The heart of restoration is the restoration of hearts.* If our hearts are not genuinely and radically restored to the Lord Jesus, then all other restoration becomes meaningless. If our hearts aren't restored to the point where we can say, "Lo, I come to do Thy will, O God," we've missed it.

> *You do not want sacrifices and offerings. Neither do You ask for whole burnt-offerings or sin-offerings. But You have accepted my offer of service for a lifetime* (Psalm 40:6).

What a revelation! He does not want the works of the fleshly man, or our sweat, or the things we do to try to please the Lord in our own way. He wants our *hearts.*

This Scripture applies again: "Because I love Jerusalem, I will continue to speak [on her behalf]. For Jerusalem's sake, I will not stop speaking. I will speak until her goodness shines like a bright light. I will speak until her salvation burns bright like a flame (Isa. 62:1). Isaiah could not rest until he could see the Church in all that it was destined to become. He prophesied it until the end, but only really saw it in the Spirit.

God wants to heal us from within. He doesn't want us walking around with our hang-ups and our fears. He doesn't want us going around with negative memories of things from our past. He doesn't want us to have to carry the weights we've carried all our lives. There is healing for the human heart. There is healing that flows from the throne of God so that God's people can be whole. That's good news! God is looking for people who will let that healing process happen to them so that they might impart it to others.

THERE IS HEALING FOR THE HUMAN HEART.

Recently, I did a study on the topic, "Be ye angry and sin not." I found some good things I could be angry at. After seeing these truths, I realized that when some things occurred, I could become angry and know it was okay. For example, I get angry when I see the followers of the occult making all kinds of headway in the world, accumulating many converts and leading them down the pathway to hell.

The enemy is doing the same thing in some of today's rock-and-roll music. The powers of the occult and the powers of the enemy are unleashed through much of this type of music. Many of the musicians know the power of satan, and they call upon it. They're not afraid to call upon hell's power. They're not afraid to wreck another person's life with the power of satan, just so they can attain their ends.

All too often, God's people are so namby-pamby. They fight over what God can do and they fight over what He can't do. Sometimes it leaves me thinking, "God, where are *your* people? Where are your people who will stand in the gap and declare the power of God over the power of the devil? Where are the ones who will declare that our God is greater than the powers of hell?" Instead of joining together to stand against the powers of darkness, we stand around fighting over whether we should be baptized in the Holy Ghost, while the baptism of filth is taking this whole world to the pit.

A Day of Power

God wants this to be a day of power. It is a day of intense out-pouring. There is warfare in the heavenlies! Paul says that "For our fight we are not using weapons which come from this world. No, our weapons come from God. They are powerful enough to break down strong forts" (2 Cor. 10:4). What kind of strongholds can we tear down when we weaken God's Word to the point of ineffectiveness? What kind of strongholds can we tear down, what kind of kingdoms can we turn into the Kingdoms of our God when we don't even realize that there is power in what God has done for us? There's *nothing we can do.* We're "blown away by the winds of false teaching..." (Eph. 4:14) or led astray by the carnality of our own minds. We let people throw Scriptures at us that cause us to stumble and fall and keep us weak.

God is calling us out of all that. He's saying that power is coming to supply strength and salvation to people who will be able to call on God and only to those people who will do so. These people won't limit God by saying, "God can't do this!" or "God can't do that!"

There's no way we can fight the forces and powers of this world or make any headway as long as we try to *naturalize* God and reduce Him to a quiet melody on a Sunday morning that has little meaning. We need the power of God planted so deeply in our lives that we can *stand* in the evil day. In that soon-coming day we will need God's power to keep us from being tossed to and fro and from being broken by every wind of doctrine.

> WE NEED THE POWER OF GOD PLANTED
> SO DEEPLY IN OUR LIVES THAT WE CAN
> *STAND* IN THE EVIL DAY.

When somebody doesn't agree with your approach and throws a Scripture at you and says, "But, brother, you can't do that," remember that when people put a stumbling block in front of you that causes you to reject something God has for you, they're in sin.

> *Jesus said to His followers, "Things will surely occur which will cause people to sin, but it will be horrible for the person who causes this to happen. If he causes one of these little ones to sin, it would be better for him to drown with a big rock tied to his neck (Luke 17:1-2).*

Would to God that He would rend the heavens and come down upon us! Just as powerfully, would to God that we would let Him change us from within, that we would be able to accept the powers that have already come from Him, walking confidently yet humbly in His Manifest Presence.

I'm not a mystic who spends ninety percent of his time on some cloud in the heavenlies. I live and work in this world. But I can say, "In Him I live, and move and have my being" (see Acts 17:28 KJV). Right now, more than anything else, we need to be people who are *in* Him, who move in Him and have our being in Him.

> *Our fight is not against human beings. No, it is against rulers, against authorities, against world powers of this darkness, and against evil spiritual beings in the heavenly world. This is why you must take up all of God's armor. Then when the time for*

battle comes, you will be able to resist. And after you have fought your best, you will stand (Ephesians 6:12-13).

Cheap Grace

*But he certainly took our suffering upon himself, and he felt our pain for us. We saw his suffering. We thought that God was punishing him. But he was wounded for the things that **we** did wrong. He was crushed for the evil things we did. The punishment, which made us well, was given to Him. And, we are healed because of **His** wounds (Isaiah 53:4-5).*

What is God's salvation? He saved us: body, soul, and spirit. He died that we might be whole—body, soul, and spirit. "But He was pierced through for our transgressions, He was crushed for our iniquities"—that takes care of our spirit. "The chastening for our well-being fell upon Him"—that takes care of our soul, or our emotional make-up. "By His scourging we are healed"—that takes care of our body. That one verse contains the entire redemptive work in a nutshell.

On the Cross Jesus provided all that was necessary to heal us—body, soul, and spirit. He wants us to be whole. He wants us to be equipped. We're not to be a Church that comes up with fifteen reasons why we're not healed, but fifteen reasons why we should be. We're not to make excuses for our own lack, but to gain strength so that there is no lack, so we can impart life to others.

We are living in perilous times, and God is reaching down in the deepest recesses of our hearts to begin healing us and making us whole so that we may do His will in the power of His Presence.

Years ago, my little boy, Donald, was in the kitchen while his mom was baking cookies. She pulled the cookie sheet out of the oven, set it on top of the stove and said, "Now, Donnie, don't touch. It's hot." She walked out of the kitchen. The temptation of those chocolate chip cookies was just too much for him. He reached up and tried to take one, and he burned his arm slightly. For a month after the incident, every time he saw that cookie sheet, he would put his hand on his arm.

This kind of response is true of us in the spiritual realm as well. When we are scarred in our emotions, unless Jesus is allowed to heal us, our entire lives will remain affected by that scar. Every fear, every hang-up, every hassle we struggle with, stays with us until the Lord Jesus is able to touch it. In our hearts, way down deep inside of us, there is a realm nobody's ever seen. It's like a box. No one has ever seen inside that box except you and God. It's the little box into which we stuff everything we don't want anybody to see.

> THE VERY HEART OF WHAT GOD IS DOING IS THE RESTORATION OF OUR HEARTS TO-WARD HIM.

It is frequently dismaying to see people I counsel with choosing to stay hurt. They don't seem to know that there's healing at the Cross. They don't seem to know that part of the salvation Jesus purchased was healing of the inner man, healing of the torment of the mind. He wants to heal us so He can commission us for service. The very heart of what God is doing is the restoration of our hearts toward Him.

So, I will give their wives to other men. I will give their fields to new owners. Everyone, from the least important to the most important, is greedy for money. Even the so-called "prophets" and "priests"—all of them tell lies (Jeremiah 8:10).

This is a declaration of a carnal ministry. The priests heal the people just enough to keep them in church, but they are not really whole. The Lord's judgment is against them. "They try to heal My people's serious injuries as if they were small wounds. They say: 'It's all right! It's all right!' But really, it's *not* all right" (Jer. 8:11).

I was born and raised as a Catholic. God opened my eyes one day to know that there was something more than the confessional. Once I went in to confess some of my sins, and the priest said, "They're not sins. Don't worry about them." Well, I walked out of there and said to myself, "He's supposed to be the priest, and he's telling me I'm okay and I know I'm not okay!" It was then that I started my search for the reality of God.

"Know this: There will be hard times during the last days" (2 Tim. 3:1). The Scriptures also tell us there will be people who have "a form of godliness" but deny its power, tying God's hands. They will do anything to keep Him under control. The attitude of these folks is, "Let's make God more understandable here," so they box Him up tightly so that they can "keep a handle on Him."

The Lord "rent" the curtain separating the Holy Place from the Most Holy Place in the Temple "from top to bottom" on that first Good Friday (see Matt. 27:51). Ever since that time, people have tried to sew it back up by saying what God can do and what He can't do, what He will do and what He won't do. Actually, the historian Josephus records that the Jews indeed sewed up the curtain that God

176

Himself had torn. Let me assure you, He never intended it to be that way. "'They should be ashamed of the terrible way they act. But they are not ashamed at all! They do not even know how to blush about their sins. So, they will fall, along with everyone else. They will be thrown to the ground when I punish them,' says the Always-Present One" (Jer. 8:12).

> *So, be happy, O you people of Jerusalem. Be joyful in the Always-Present One, your God. He will do what is right, and He will give you the autumn rains. He will send you abundant showers, both the autumn rain and the spring rains, as before. And the threshing-floors will be full of wheat. And, the barrels will overflow with new wine and olive oil* (Joel 2:23-24).

The Vats Shall Overflow

Joel was an end-time prophet of the Lord. He could see into the heavens and declare those things that were to come to mortal man. Do you think he was concerned with how much wheat would be gathered in from an agricultural harvest? Do you think he was concerned with how much wine and oil would be stockpiled? Joel was speaking prophetically to us in our generation. He was speaking to *us*, not to the farmers who lived around him.

"And the threshing-floors will be full of wheat" (Joel 2:24). The wheat makes bread; bread is the type of the Word, the bread of life, the living Word of the Lord. When the Lord restores His people and restores His Church, we'll be abounding in wheat. There will be living bread for everybody, not just another Bible study. In that day, there will be bread for everyone. Everyone will be satisfied in their spirits. Everyone will be nourished, cared for, and strengthened the way they need it. "And the barrels will overflow with new wine and olive oil" (Joel 2:24). It will be the wine of the Holy Spirit and the oil of gladness. We'll be overflowing with wine and oil! Glory to God! It will be there in abundance: God's blessing, God's restoration of His people.

"The Always-Present One says, 'Your thoughts are not like My thoughts. Your ways are not like My ways" (Isa. 55:8). If we could take the brain matter that has existed in every person who ever lived on the face of the earth, from Adam until now, and we could somehow put that intellect together and construct one massive brain for humanity, do you know what God would say? "My thoughts are still higher than your thoughts, and My ways are still not your ways."

He's been in existence from eternity past. He'll be in existence throughout eternity future. He's dealt with the likes of Moses and Abraham. He has dealt with the kings and the judges and the prophets. He has dealt with the ministries of the early Church. He is the almighty God of the vast universe! Then there's us! We "bopped onto the scene" 25, 35, 45 or more years ago, and we think we know what we're doing. Isn't it a little ridiculous? We tie Him up by limiting God according to our own way of thinking.

"I was the One who sent My great 'army' against you people. Those swarming locusts and the hopping locusts, the stripping locusts and the gnawing locusts ate up your crops. However, I will make it up to you for those bad years" (Joel 2:25). The locust and the cankerworm and the palmerworm and the caterpillar are all different stages of development of the same insect: the locust. One eats the root of the plant. Another eats the stem. The third eats the leaves. And finally, the locust eats everything in sight. What does that leave? Nothing. This is Joel's declaration to what we have done to the Church with our complacency, lethargy, and carelessness. We have allowed the palmerworm, the cankerworm, the caterpillar, and the locust to eat everything until nothing remains.

But the promise of God is, "I will restore all that lethargy has eaten away and all that complacency has eaten away and all that carnality has done." How we've limited God! Let's flee to His Presence where real restoration is accomplished.

In John 4 we read the story of the woman at the well. The woman at the well said to Jesus, "Sir, I now understand that you are a prophet. Our ancestors worshiped on this mountain, but you Jews say that Jerusalem is the place where people must worship." And Jesus said to her, "Believe me, woman, the time is coming when you won't worship the Father on this mountain or in Jerusalem. You Samaritans are worshiping that which you don't understand, but we Jews are worshiping what we know. Salvation comes from the Jewish people. But the time is coming and has now come when the true worshipers will worship the Father in the true, spiritual way. The Father is searching for this kind of people to worship Him" (John 4:19-23).

True worshipers will worship in His Presence. It becomes their life to worship and experience His Manifest Presence.

God is seeking. His Spirit is going "to and fro" across the earth, brooding upon the earth, looking for true worshipers, looking for those who will worship Him in Spirit and in truth.

"God is Spirit." Jesus went on to say, "The people who worship God must worship Him in the true way and with the right spirit" (John 4:24).

God is looking for a people who will worship Him in spirit and in truth, a people who won't limit Him, a people who won't put a bag over His head. Or put a bag over their own heads and say, "I don't see it. That's not right. God doesn't work that way."

Repentance

Jesus said, "I am taking a trip to prepare a place for you" (John 14:2). He wasn't making split-level condominiums for us; He was preparing a place in the Spirit for us. "So that," He says, "where I am you might also be," in spirit. If we're going to worship God, we have to worship in spirit and in truth. There can be no limitations, no hesitation. This place in the spirit is the place of His fullness—His Manifest Presence.

The River of the Water of Life

"The angel showed me a river of fresh water. It sparkled like crystal. It flowed from God's throne and from the Lamb's throne" (Rev. 22:1).

When we approach the throne of God, what comes forth? It is the river of the water of life. That means if I go to His Presence to worship Him, I will be bathed in the river of the water of life that proceeds from the throne of God, flowing clear as crystal. If we want to be energized and motivated and controlled by His life so that we overflow with His love, His power, and His character, we need to go before His Presence. In His Presence, the river of the water of life flows, and this is what we need.

God is restoring the hearts of His people. The healing of our hearts takes place in God's Presence. It is there that we find the power to change and all the blessings God has for us, including the wholeness He has for us. How we need to *live* in His presence. How desperately we need His Manifest Presence!

> ## THE HEALING OF OUR HEARTS TAKES PLACE IN GOD'S PRESENCE.

We frequently get so bogged down in tradition and the letter of the Law that we forget that the letter kills, but the Spirit gives life (see 2 Cor. 3:6). We forget what Jesus said to the Scribes and Pharisees when He looked them square in the eyes and said, "You people search the Scriptures, because in the Scriptures you think you have life. But the Scriptures point to Me" (John 5:39—author's paraphrase).

When the Word of God is energized by the life of God, and it's taken by the Holy Spirit and etched upon our hearts, life is imparted.

If you're not filled with the Holy Spirit, you need to be filled. If that is your case, did you ever wonder why you're struggling so hard sometimes? It is because you were never meant to live your Christian life apart from the empowering of the Holy Spirit. Likewise, if you've never been baptized in water for the circumcision of heart and the change that God wants to bring about within you, no wonder you struggle.

"O One Who Is Always Present of the armies [of heaven], how lovely is Your dwelling-place! I really want to be there in the courtyards of the Always-Present One. My whole being shouts for joy to the living God!" (Ps. 84:1-2). Does your soul long and yearn for the courts of the Lord? Are you satisfied with what you have? I've been saved, baptized, filled with the Holy Ghost for 17 years, and I still long for more of His Presence and more of His love and more of His anointing.

It's not something I do in myself. It's not something I force myself to do, but His mercies are new every morning. His keeping power far surpasses my own carnality and my own understanding.

How did the Psalmist know how lovely the dwelling places of the Lord were unless he had been there? "I really want to be there in the courtyards of the Always-Present One. My whole being shouts for joy to the living God! Happy are those who dwell in Your house. They are always praising You" (Ps. 84:2,4). God does not want to have a bride who visits Him only on weekends, but to have a people who will dwell in His house permanently in His Spirit.

Dwelling in the house of the Lord keeps us free from the stain of sin in day-to-day life.

"Happy is the person whose strength is in You. Such an individual truly wants to go on a pilgrimage in their hearts" (Ps. 84:5). Have you allowed God to etch upon your heart the highways to Zion? Have you allowed Him to get down to where you really live? Have you allowed Him to turn that stony heart into a heart of flesh?

If you are willing, God will take you into His purpose. If you are willing, you can discover a dimension of fellowship and intimacy beyond your imagination. There is a fullness and sonship that yet awaits those who earnestly want Him and are willing to pay the price necessary to walk in the Manifest Presence of God.

God's plan and passion is to manifest Himself in the earth through a pure and submitted people. This desire has never changed.

182

He will marry His wisdom and holiness to genuine praise, worship, and personal intimacy in our hearts. There, His Manifest Presence will become evident to a dying world. So follow your heart! Yield to the burning desire within you to be all God wants you to be. Say, "Yes, Lord!" with great abandonment and confidence. Put yourself under the mercy and grace of God and pray, "All I am, all I have, all I hope and dream to do is yours. Do with me as you will, that I might fulfill all your desire for me. Forgive me for wanting my own way. Lead me in Your path without fear. I trust in thee."

> GOD'S PLAN AND PASSION IS TO MANIFEST HIMSELF IN THE EARTH THROUGH A PURE AND SUBMITTED PEOPLE.

Now wait upon the Lord daily, yielding to Him in prayer and see if God doesn't prove to be true to His Word! See for yourself if a whole new theater of God's Kingdom doesn't unfold before you as He leads you deeper into Himself—His Manifest Presence.

Presence Ponderings

1. God did not lead us out of the kingdom of darkness to abandon us, but to plant us firmly in His Kingdom of Light.

2. If our hearts are not restored to serve God selflessly, then our service becomes in vain; God wants to heal and commission us for His service.

3. God will restore unto us all that the worms of complacency have eaten away, but we must first retreat into His Presence.

4. The plan of God is to manifest His Presence throughout the earth; this has always been His plan, and it forever will be.

Epilogue

All of us have uncovered faces; we reflect the same glory. It comes from the Spirit of the Lord. With one glory after another, we are being changed to look more like Him (2 Corinthians 3:18).

The search for His Manifest Presence was kindled in my heart many years ago. After I had been a Christian for 12 years, something in my heart said, "There is more to serving the Lord than what we have experienced. There is more to this thing called Christianity than meets the eye." I had the uncanny feeling that all we had touched and all we had experienced was merely the tip of the iceberg. In the depths of my heart, I knew there was much more to experience. I have searched for His fullness. I have found a depth in God. I see a depth of relationship and experience that God wants for us that we have never seen before. There is a light, a revelation, a closeness with Him that He yet beckons us to experience. It's on the other side of the Cross—the other side of purity, the other side of brokenness, the other side of abandonment. It's there for you and me to experience, that we might behold with un-veiled face the glory of the Lord and the face of Jesus Christ.

The Lord Jesus declared, "You are my friend, if you do what I tell you to do. I am no longer calling you 'slaves,' because a slave doesn't know what his master is doing. I am calling you 'friends,' because I have revealed to you everything which I have heard from my Father" (John 15:14-15). He still is looking for men and women that He can call His friends. He is calling us into the most holy place where true fellowship and intimacy begin, where there is a sense of His Presence that goes beyond the realm of faith, passes through faith and is touched in genuine reality. He wants to bring us to that place where the Word becomes flesh and our fellowship is truly with the living God, not based merely on the written Word of God, but proven in the experience of our daily lives. There is a union with God that yet awaits all believers who will but go after that place in God.

But this people is a remnant people. It's not all of Abraham's seed that experiences it, nor is it all of Isaac's seed. It's those born of Jacob who have wrestled with the angel and have had their names changed. These are the people who are broken and selfless, whose only burning passion is to bring pleasure and honor and glory to the Lord Jesus Christ. This place of intimacy is reserved for those who are on the other side of the veil. And the cry of the Spirit is to come up hither. "Come up hither, that you might expe-rience that place that I prepared for you when I went to the Father." There is a place of fellowship that goes deeper than the gifts; there's a place of fellowship that goes deeper than ministry; there is a knowing and a wisdom that goes beyond that which we are touched by in the baptism of the Holy Spirit. There is the depth of

His fullness that the heart of God calls us to experience in Him, that we might be a people who do not know just in part, nor prophesy in part, but know fully, even as we are known (see 1 Cor. 13:9-10). We can be a people who no longer see in a mirror darkly, but see face-to-face; a people who have laid aside the childish things to be able to handle the glorious things of mature sonship.

There is yet a Jeremiah 31 experience for us. God has a new covenant for His people, a covenant in which God's laws are written in our hearts. His ways are planted within us, that He might truly be our God and that we might be His people; that we would all know Him, from the least to the greatest. He wants us to experience, not a superficial knowing, not a superficial acquaintance, but a deep, abiding, intimate knowing, even as a husband knows his wife in their most intimate times.

His Manifest Presence is our place of safety, our place of protection. His Manifest Presence is our place of change, our place of restoration. His Manifest Presence in the sanctuary is our place of ministry, where the world sees Christ, not a doctrine, not a system, not a church, not a theology.

But the world sees Christ when Christ is permitted to show Himself through yielded, broken vessels. The Lord will manifest Himself, His glorious Presence, to and through a people who are thus committed to Him.

How else could the Psalmist say, "You will show me the pathway to life. Being with You will fill me with joy. At Your right hand, I will find pleasure forever" (Ps. 16:11) unless he had experienced the glory of His Manifest Presence? How could David cry out, "Because You are my Help, I will gladly sing of Your protection" (Ps. 63:7) unless he had experienced such intimacy? The prophet Isaiah saw into these last days and in the fourth chapter of his book he said,

> *The Always-Present One will wash away the filth from the women of Jerusalem. He will wash the bloodstains out of Jerusalem. He will cleanse Jerusalem with the spirit of fairness and the spirit of fire. As the Always-Present One did when Israel left Egypt, He will cover them with a cloud of smoke during the day. And, He will cover them with a bright flaming fire at night. These proofs will be over Mount Zion. They will be over every meeting of the people there. There will be a covering over every person. This covering will be a place of safety. It will protect the people from the heat of the sun. It will be a safe place to hide from the storm and rain* (Isaiah 4:4-6).

Isaiah the prophet saw the last-day manifestation of God's Presence in a way that was even more glorious than what Moses and the children of Israel experienced when they came out of Egypt.

This, then, is what our hearts should be set on—to pursue Him with all that is within us, with all our soul, with all our might, and with all our strength. Not to be content with the gifts of the Spirit, not to be content with that which He can bless us with, not even to be content with the blessings of ministry, of calling, of talents or abilities. But our one abiding passion is to be satisfied with nothing less than Him. From David's Tabernacle to Solomon's Temple, there was nothing in the Ark except His laws written on stone. There will be a people who are so abandoned to Him that there will be nothing in their hearts, no preconceived motives, no gifts, no ministries, that takes a higher place than the ecstasy of a true personal relationship with the living God. The arms of the Lord God are stretched out to us and He beckons us to come unto Him.

Additional copies of this book and other
book titles from DESTINY IMAGE are
available at your local bookstore.

Call toll-free: 1-800-722-6774.

Send a request for a catalog to:

Destiny Image® Publishers, Inc.

P.O. Box 310
Shippensburg, PA 17257-0310

*"Speaking to the Purposes of God for This
Generation and for the Generations to Come."*

**For a complete list of our titles,
visit us at www.destinyimage.com.**